Why Did I Walk into This Room?

Why Did I Walk into This Room?

A Thinking Person's Guide to Growing Older

∾

KENNEY F. HEGLAND
was a James E. Rogers Professor Emeritus of Law
University of Arizona James E. Rogers College of Law

LAWRENCE FROLIK
Professor of Law Emeritus
University of Pittsburgh School of Law

CAROLINA ACADEMIC PRESS
Durham, North Carolina

Library of Congress Cataloging-in-Publication Data

Names: Hegland, Kenney F., 1940– author. | Frolik,
    Lawrence A., author.
Title: Why did I walk into this room? : a thinking person's
    guide to growing older / by Kenney F. Hegland, Lawrence
    Frolik.
Description: Durham, North Carolina : Carolina Academic
    Press, LLC, [2020]
Identifiers: LCCN 2020027785 (print) | LCCN 2020027786
    (ebook) | ISBN 9781531019761 (paperback) |
    ISBN 9781531019778 (ebook)
Subjects: LCSH: Retirement—Planning, | Aging—Social
    aspects. | Aging—Economic aspects.
Classification: LCC HQ1062 .H354 2020 (print) |
    LCC HQ1062 (ebook) | DDC 305.26—dc23
LC record available at https://lccn.loc.gov/2020027785
LC ebook record available at https://lccn.loc.gov/2020027786

Carolina Academic Press
700 Kent Street
Durham, North Carolina 27701
Telephone (919) 489-7486 | Fax (919) 493-5668
www.cap-press.com

Printed in the United States of America

To Boomers

Will they still need you?
Will they still feed you?
Now you're 64 (more or less)

While the sun and moon endure
Luck's a chance, but trouble's sure,
I'd face it as a wise man would,
And train for ill and not for good.

—A.E. HOUSMAN

I'll make up for the sobriety of my youth,
I shall go out in my slippers in the rain
And pick flowers in other people's gardens
And learn to spit . . .

—JENNY JOSEPH

Contents

PART THREE
SLINGS AND ARROWS

PART FOUR
SLOWING DOWN TIME'S WINGED CHARIOT

PART FIVE
MONEY AND HEALTH WOES

PART SIX
MENTAL ILLNESS

PART SEVEN
CARE GIVING

PART EIGHT
PREPARING FOR THE WORST OF TIMES

PART NINE
THE FINAL CURTAIN

Foreword

After the completion of this book, but before its publication, Kenney Hegland died. Kenney was very bright with a keen understanding of aging. He had a great sense of humor and never took himself too seriously. His writings and life expressed his desire to be of service to others. He will be missed.

—L.F.

Acknowledgments

Robert Fleming, who shared so much of his knowledge, Barbara Sattler, John Jefferies, Caleb Hegland, wonderful editors, and the folks at Marie Trump's writing group: Ann Hammond, Beverly King Pollock, Beth Smith, Bob Samuels, Lorna Garrod, Bill Lofquist, Linda Greeley, Mary Ann Presman, Terry Tanner, Ted Glinski, and our dear friend, Roselyn Schiffman.

Preface

This isn't a "how to do it" book, it's a "how to think about it" book. We won't treat you as someone in need of instruction. We respect your intelligence. We'll treat you as a good friend we can help by sharing what we have learned over the years.

We know the problems you and your family will face, and we'll suggest both legal and practical solutions. Aging isn't for sissies and it's much more than:

"I probably need a will. I'll get around to it."

We'll alert you to the things that will go wrong, suggest ways to avoid them, and what to do if you didn't. It's heavy stuff, but we'll lighten the load with existential musing and fairly good jokes (at least we think they are).

Along the way you'll hear from doctors, read a few poems, learn a little law, and love brief appearances from the likes of Edna St. Vincent Millay, Charles Dickens, John Keats, the Beatles, and Jay Leno. We won't have you putting down our book.

Skim the stuff below; we cover a lot. Do four critical things: make your house safe, check your blood pressure, talk to your loved ones about the elephant, and learn new things — and you've made a good start.

Here is a quick overview.

PART ONE
THE AARP LETTER AND BEYOND

What to expect as you age, what to consider if you're retiring, and what to do if you're bored. Making your home safe and considering a retirement facility. Most important of all, the elephant.

PART TWO
THE GOOD NEWS

Sex. Grandkids (raising them, educational trusts). Remarriage (the triumph of hope over experience). As lawyers we know a thing or two; we'll cover divorce.

PART THREE
SLINGS AND ARROWS

Hearing loss, bad meds, insomnia, and opioids. Driving. Age and disability discrimination. Dealing with doctors, surgeons, and lawyers. On a far more important note, protecting your loved ones from abuse.

PART FOUR
SLOWING TIME'S WINGED CHARIOT

Exercise. Supplements and diets. Strokes and the danger of high blood pressure.

PART FIVE
MONEY AND HEALTH WOES

Social Security, Medicare, being house rich and cash poor, and reverse mortgages.

PART SIX
MENTAL ILLNESS

Scary senior moments, actual dementia, depression, and guardianships.

PART SEVEN
CARE GIVING

Deciding and caring for others, and nursing homes.

PART EIGHT
PREPARING FOR THE WORST OF TIMES

Estate planning, avoiding probate, living trusts, and health care directives.

PART NINE
THE FINAL CURTAIN

Death in the family, probate, pulling plugs, death with dignity, hospice, mourning.

∽

"Isn't there something to help us through all of these problems?" In 1785 John Quincy Adams, destined to be our sixth president, entered Harvard. He hoped to learn the Ultimate Generalization, the one that would explain everything. He was disappointed. We all need good advice. The Ultimate Advice, the one that always helps, is inspired by Dylan Thomas:

> *Time held me green and dying,*
> *Though I sang in my chains like the sea.*

Time holds all of us, if not green and dying. So what? *Let's sing.*

Part One

~

The AARP Letter and Beyond

1

What to Expect

*Waitresses will call you "dear" and gangbangers
will give you their seats.*

There are a lot of positives about growing older but we'll save them until the end, after we have depressed you for several pages.

You'll lose strength, flexibility, balance, and stamina; you'll lose some memory and, like old dogs, you won't be able to learn new tricks as quickly. As for computers, ask your grandkids.

Add to these slings and arrows, going to reunions only to discover that none of your classmates have come, only their grandparents. And looking in the mirror isn't a piece of cake.

You'll cut easily, and your face will wrinkle. Why? Fewer cells. Babies are so cute, so plump, so lovable because they are bundles of cells. Cut them, and they heal instantly. Over time, cells die.

Along with cell loss comes a general decline in physical prowess — heart and lung capacity shrink. Gray hair? Beginning around age 30 hair follicles produce hydrogen peroxide, blocking the follicles' ability to make melanin, the pigment that gives hair its color. (In a terribly misguided apology, Mother Nature tries to make up by sprouting vast amounts of hair on your ears.)

Loss of balance. We're not talking about watching only the cable channel you agree with and smiling to learn why you're right.

We're talking avoiding falls. They are very serious at our age, leading to broken hips and hospitalization. Low blood pressure (usually a blessing) is a common cause. Exercise, personal trainers, canes and walkers are better than broken hips.

Weight gain. Metabolism slows. Looking at old folks (who we now define as anyone a few months older than us), it seems old folks get skinny. But they were *always* skinny. Generational comparisons can mislead; sure there are skinny old folks but they were skinny when they were young. Most of us are doomed to gain weight. But how much you gain, well, that is up to you.

Hearing and vision. How often do you nod in agreement even though you have no idea what your dinner companion said? ("Looks like you're putting on a few pounds.") The high price of hearing aids is no longer an excuse; much cheaper ones can be purchased online or in stores like Target.

Bad vision makes driving a crapshoot, and both bad vision and hearing increase likely falls.

Sex. Viagra attests that sex is well and thriving. In nursing homes this presents something of a problem (or something of a benefit).

Memory loss. "Why did I come into the kitchen?" "What is the name of my dentist?" "When you keep forgetting things, what do they call that?"

Not to panic. You've been having "senior moments" your whole life and they don't often lead to severe memory loss. Chances are you'll remain mentally active in advanced old age despite occasional lapses.

Personality changes. Getting grumpy? Maybe. Discomfort trumps charm; small talk is hard if you're worried about your next doctor's appointment. Put on a happy face even if you don't mean it.

Becoming more dogmatic? More set on your views? The world is changing so fast you might retreat to known truths. But many go in the opposition direction, realizing how little they know and that they're the same old fool they always were.

The rise and fall of old folks. We used to be special, valued, dignified, tellers of wonderful stories, teachers of deep wisdom and, in times of trouble, providers of wise counsel and comfort. What happened?

Wise? Madison Avenue has convinced us that gray hair and wrinkles are not the signs of wisdom but are simply ugly. Thanks to terrific advances in public health and medicine, we're no longer rare, we're everywhere, crowding the malls, taking our sweet time turning left, and bankrupting Social Security. As to our knowledge and wisdom, we've published everything we have to say.

OK, Boomer. To add insult to injury millennials wave off our sound advice with "OK, Boomer." They're blaming our generation for everything wrong in the world. Not to be too defensive, but we did make substantial progress in ending world poverty (not much of an issue for middle-class millennials), led the Civil Rights Movement (which millennials may have heard of), and have made great advances in medicine (assuring that millennials will live long enough to be attacked by *their* grandchildren). They're spot on, however, when it comes to global warming.

Now the promised good news. You'll live longer; at the age 65 men have another 18 years, women 20, and the negatives don't suddenly show up, they sneak up and you get used to them. We tend to think good things will be better than they turn out to be (think of being disappointed with highly praised movies) and we tend to think bad things will be worse than they turn out to be. Is growing old insufferable? Nope.

Studies have shown that older folks are happier than younger ones. Pity those upstarts who cut in front of you in the checkout line in order not to be late for work, school, or a job interview.

Why not be happy? Free from the restraints of adulthood, no longer the frowning teacher enforcing rules, you're the kid swinging too high. Free to sleep in, wear a purple ribbon in your hair, never tie a tie, eat a peach, and disturb the universe — or at least your neighbors.

While we have your attention, a quick overview to keep you playing. We cover them more in later chapters.

- Check your blood pressure. Hypertension is a leading cause of strokes and is known as the "silent killer" — folks don't know they have it. Check!
- Make your home safe; a broken hip is a bummer.
- Keep friends, keep active, and keep dogs (okay, cats too).
- Try new things, like clubs, classes, and pickleball.
- Eat right, at least in front of your family.
- Let no potbelly evade your eyes, exercise. Don't just hide those sagging triceps, exercise. It improves your physical and mental health and holds back depression. Thirty minutes of walking, not even all at once, is the gold standard. A Harvard professor says the best kinds of exercise are walking, swimming, Tai Chi, weights, and, you probably didn't guess, Kegels.
- The Harvard Medical School is particularly high on Tai Chi, saying it improves balance, helps flexibility, reduces pain, strengthens the heart, and reduces stress. Yoga is also good if you can still get up off the floor.
- Read this book. No joke.

2

Retire?

Take this job and shove it, I ain't
working here no more.

Even if you have the verbal flare of Johnny Paycheck, this isn't the best of exit lines.

Work never has been just a paycheck. It's a sense of self-worth, it's daily challenges, it's friends, and it's a reason to get out of bed in the morning. Don't pull the plug too quickly.

If you retire, what are you going to do? Buying a Winnebago and touring America sounds wonderful, but for how long? Sure you want to spend more time with your grandchildren, but soon they'll be teenagers with nose rings.

But there's no reason to keep working just because you don't know what you'll do in retirement. There are scads of opportunities; you may find a whole new you, a new sense of worth, new daily decisions, and new friends. Learning new things keeps one spry. We'll make suggestions in the next chapter.

Money. How much will you need, where will you get it, and don't forget the cost of medical insurance and medical care.

The traditional advice is that you'll need 70% to 80% of what you made before during your retirement, and financial advisers say, to play it safe, you'll need $500,000 in savings or investments. Good luck with that.

Making a list of expenses is important. There are books and websites to help. Don't overlook the new costs you will encounter. A major new expense is health insurance. Some continue to work just to remain on their employer's health plan, at least until they are 65 and can qualify for Medicare. Unfortunately, there is the possibility of needing long-term care; *it's not covered by Medicare.*

There will be savings. No buying work clothes, less dry cleaning. Less valium.

Where will you get the money? Here a quick overview of pensions, IRAs, and Social Security. More in later chapters.

If you're retiring from a firm that has a pension plan talk to its human resources people about your options, a *life-time pension* or a *lump-sum payout.* The problem with pensions is that they end when you do (sorry) so you'll have nothing to leave the kids. Also the monthly payments do not increase with inflation; your purchasing power drops. Lump-sum payouts create major tax problems, but they can be avoided, so talk to an accountant or financial advisor.

As for Social Security, your main choice will be when to take it, early (age 62), at full retirement (around age 66), or late (age 70). Go to the Social Security website to see when you qualify for benefits and how much you will get. If you take early retirement and go on working, not only will you have lower Social Security monthly payments, your benefit will be reduced $1 for every $2 you make over $17,000. Don't do it, That's a definite no-no. When you get to your full retirement age there are no reductions no matter how much you earn.

If you wait till 70 your check will be at its highest, and the longer you work, the larger your check.

You're entitled to Medicare at age 65. It makes no difference if you continue to work. You qualify if you're eligible for Social Security or married to someone who is. If you're not on Social Security you can buy in. It's expensive.

There are choices to make and scare ads to ignore. Medicare Part A covers most hospital bills; they can run into the tens of thousands (and we're talking about a couple of days). Part B, which you pay for, pays for 80% of most doctor visits. One gaping hole: Medicare does not cover long-term care. Should you go with traditional Medicare or with an HMO? What about Medigap policies? Prescription coverage? We'll save all of that for later.

3

Retirement Angst

How many TV reruns can I watch?

Experiencing new things is the best way to keep the mind
young, pliable and growing—into the 90s and beyond.
DANIEL LEVITIN, neuroscientist

It may be that when we no longer know what to do
We have come our real work.
WENDELL BERRY

Mind-forg'd manacles.
WILLIAM BLAKE

Take a deep breath, pick yourself up,
Dust yourself off, and start all over again.
FRANK SINATRA

Mind-forg'd manacles. How many times have you not done something because you knew you couldn't do it even though you never tried doing it? Thinking back to life's lost opportunities will be too depressing, so let's think ahead.

Don't be too serious, too mature, too condemning of your options with "That will never work." How about starting with "Run off and join the circus"? Ignore your little voice when it says, "That's stupid." Stay with us.

Silly ideas lead to better ones. "What with animal rights they probably don't have circuses anymore, but maybe I can become a profession clown." Better still, jot down your ideas. Writing slows the mind and opens new avenues. "If not a clown maybe volunteering at the Children's Hospital. I like kids and would do a good job. I'll call."

Here's an assignment (we're teachers). Write a couple of possibilities in each category.

Work
> Full or part time, home or elsewhere
> *List your possibilities*

Learn
> Learn new stuff or new skills
> *List your possibilities*

Serve
> Volunteer
> *List your possibilities*

Create
> Write, paint, speak
> *List possibilities*

Write in the book so you can't resell it. Don't skip the assignment and read ahead to see what we have to say. What you have to say is far more important. Help us out for our next edition and send your list to Frolik@pitt.edu.

Okay, here are some hints.

CREATE

We'll start with writing because that's what we do. The best place to start is a writing group. If you're unsure what to write, you'll get a prompt:

Twenty seconds to go. Down by a point. Stiggall has the ball. He missed the last two shots.

Jane looked up. Did John really just say that he wants out of our marriage?

You don't know anything about basketball and hate family dramas? Fine. You do know about winning and losing, love and family conflict. The traditional advice is to write about what you know; try writing about what you don't know you know. What you don't know you know will come when you write about what you know. Trust us.

Stiggall's mom is in the bleachers. Things can't go worse. At breakfast John told her he wants out of the marriage.

(Sorry, cut us a little slack. Only mind-forg'd manacles insist on staying on point.)

Write about childhood friends, teachers and, why not, painful crushes. Once you start expect a flood of memories. Try a short story or — why not — a novel. Don't worry, you don't know what your novel is about; write it and find out. Stephen King doesn't plot, he starts with a scene, some characters, and sees what happens. Best line ever: "I never thought she'd marry him."

We were lousy at painting; none of our stuff made the frig. However, there are classes at community colleges and commercial places where they provide canvas, paints, and wine.

Toast Masters and similar programs get you up in front of people talking.

"Me? I could never do that, talk in front of people. I'd make a fool of myself." In grade school Jay Leno was lectured, "Stop making jokes, you'll make a fool of yourself."

Join a community theatre (too early to get an agent). There's standup comedy. A reporter who spent time at Walter Reed tells of a disfigured soldier, his face badly burned. He didn't sit around watching *Law and Order*; he dusted himself off and became a standup comic. He would begin, "I fought in Iraq twice. The second was a real blast."

LEARN

The world is so full of a number of things
I'm sure we should all be as happy as kings.

ROBERT LOUIS STEVENSON

Thanks to community colleges, books, and YouTube, you can learn things and skills you never realized you were interested in, like cooking, gardening, playing the piano, the fall of the Roman Empire, and what your dog really thinks of you. The Bernard Osher Foundation supports senior learning in 170 colleges and universities. Fun stuff. No mandatory attendance, no tests.

Book clubs are good, particularly for men (we have few friends). A short story club is very helpful if you are a slow reader. Try out the nonfiction section of your bookstore or library. There are many wonderful books, such as *Einstein's Theory of Relativity Made Easy.* Ha!

Travel is replete with educational opportunities, making plans, finding good restaurants, and learning how to say, "Where's the bathroom?" in Greek.

WORK

A Target greeter is reprimanded, "Harry you're doing a won-
derful job. People love you. But you are always late. When you
were in the Navy, what did they say when you came in late?"

"Good morning, Admiral."

Wonderful joke, important point. The admiral wants something different, no longer being the boss, no longer making critical decisions in the fog of uncertainty; he just wants to be a regular person and to make decisions that are either right or wrong; hammers are on aisle two or they aren't.

Moral: No need to be the same old you.

Finding work. Craigslist and want ads in the local paper are a good place to start. (Please subscribe.) Both your local Area

Council on Aging and the AARP have job sites, and you can find scores on the Internet.

VOLUNTEERING

*I am of the opinion that my life belongs to the whole community
and as long as I live, it is my privilege to do for it what I can.
I want to be thoroughly used up when I die, for the harder
I work, the more I will live.*

GEORGE BERNARD SHAW

Volunteering need not be full time. Often there are one-day opportunities. Try your Area Council on Aging and www.national service.gov—type in an interest (veterans, education, elderly) and zip code and, like magic, scores of possibilities appear.

One place to volunteer is to visit patients in hospice. Deep bonding often occurs, and one's fear of death is lessened. In *Final Exam* surgeon Pauline Chen writes:

Dealing with the dying allows us to nurture our best humanistic tendencies.

Turn off the TV. You know how that rerun will end and you never even liked it. Consider all of your choices. Too confusing? Fine. Wendell Berry has something to say:

The mind that is not baffled is not employed.

4

A Critical Talk: The Elephant

What if mom needs home care? Dad ran that red light.
Should I say something? Do they have enough money? They're
going to die someday. Have they planned their funeral?
What's going to happen to me?

It's easier to gossip, talk about the weather, watch TV. If you talk about some of the things that are on everyone's mind everything goes better.

We've asked our students if they ever talked with their parents about end of life. "No, we don't talk about dying in my culture." In years of teaching we haven't run across a culture that does. One student, in obvious distress, raised her hand.

"We never talked about death. When my dad died it was horrible. There were so many things I wanted to tell him. Was he proud of me? We argued over the funeral. I'm still not talking to my brother."

Starting the talk is hard. We recommend writing a letter to the family, to collect thoughts and topics; have the family read the letter and go from there. Here is one possibility with commentary.

Dear Folks,

If there comes a time I am quite sick and unable to make my own decisions, I want my family to make them for me.

While everyone should have a living will usually doctors defer to your family's wishes. This makes sense. Often living wills are filled out years before they come into play, with boxes to check. When the time comes, your family *if it knows your general wishes*, will have a better feel for the actual situation— your age, how likely the recovery, how painful and expensive the treatment, and how you're generally getting along.

If my family can't agree, it's up to Kris, who has my health care power of attorney.

We'll have more to say about health care powers of attorney downstream. Here we simply note that is probably the most important document to have.

I realize your decision might be to "pull the plug" and remove me from all life support. Nurses have assured me that dying from a lack of hydration is not a bad way to go. Keeping me alive beyond is not an act of love. Don't keep me alive simply because no one wants to face the bad news. Be brave.

Insist that my doctors tell you my chances of recovery, how long it would take, and what would be my condition afterwards. A good question to ask, "Would it surprise you if he died in the next month?"

Doctors are reluctant to give bad news, perhaps fearing the self-filling prophecy. In Oscar Wilde's play *The Importance of Being Earnest*, Earnest's aunt is told that he had died after his doctor had given him only "a short time to live." Her response? "He seems to have had great confidence in the opinion of his physician."

I can live without walking but don't want to live if I can no longer appreciate my family and friends and can no longer understand the world around me.

This is a good time to reflect on life. Dr. Jerome Groopman, in

How Doctors Think, cautions against focusing only on the negative consequences of disability, on what will be lost after colostomy, prostrate surgery, mastectomy. *This neglects our extraordinary capacity to enjoy life with less than "perfect" health.*

> *I'm a wimp when it comes to pain. Tell my doctors to give me enough pain meds even if it means they might kill me; that's my choice and my family supports it.*
>
> *If there comes a time that my driving endangers others, tell me. I'll be mad, but I don't want to end my life by killing someone. And I was always a better driver than you kids.*
>
> *If there comes a time that I must move in with one of you, I want the others to realize how difficult and expensive my care will be. They should also take turns giving the caregiver some time off.*

Caring for disabled relatives is extremely hard and quite expensive. Far too often family members not involved in the care complain that the caregiver is wasting money.

> *Families fight over who gets the grandfather clock. Get together and write a list of who gets what. I know you will value things differently. It would be great to talk about what you want and why you want it. Wonderful family stories and family memories loom.*

The grandfather clock is a metaphor. Lawyers agree that most bitter family fights are not about money but about who gets family heirlooms. *Written lists* avoid "She said" "No she didn't."

> *My will is with my lawyer, Robert Fleming. My other important papers are in the desk, the one next to the grandfather clock.*
>
> *I want to die at home or in a hospice. Short stays in ICU are okay to stabilize my condition and figure out what to do. Donate what you can of me.*

We'll have a lot to say about hospice. For now three quick things: it is not just for cancer patients, it can be done at home, and some people get better and walk away. Far too many never avail themselves of hospice or wait until the last weeks of life.

As to burial, I want cremation and an Irish Wake. I've been thinking about my death. I've made peace with it and am no longer afraid. My life seems to be going better.

Morrie, in *Tuesdays with Morrie*, after telling us growing old isn't so bad, reminds us of what so many wise people have told us: life gets a lot better if you overcome the fear of death.

We've just read about creating a *"When I die"* file—not *"If I die"* but *"When I die."* It should contain your passwords, will, bank accounts, funeral instructions, letters to loved ones and, if you wrote one, your letter. The file will save your family much confusion.

Talking about the elephant—your death—isn't grim. Once it starts expect laughs and memories. Remember your A.E. Housman:

> *Malt does more than Milton can,*
> *To justify God's ways to man.*

5

Making Your Home Safe

When younger, the bedroom, now, the bathroom.

"Have you had any falls in the last year?" the nurse smiles.

Falls are serious. Prevent them. Are rugs secure? Rugs need sticky rubber backing, and yet they should be thin enough to make it easy to navigate over them—even with a cane, walker, or just heavy feet. Or just get rid of them. Does the shower have slip-proof mats? Grab bars? Professionally installed are best; see a surgical supply company for referral. Light-weight tables flip when used to help get up. Are there toys (grandkids' or pets') on the floor?

You'll lose night vision. Are there enough nightlights to get from bed to bath?

You'll lose strength. Do the chairs have arms to help with getting up? Are there grab bars near the toilet and bath? Is the toilet seat height raised?

Your reaction times lessen. Is the water heater set so that it will douse you with scalding water?

You may lose track of time. Large clocks in each room help orient. Or just ask Alexa.

You may have an emergency. Do you have smoke and carbon monoxide detectors? Are phones accessible? Use cordless phones if not cell phones—ones with big keys. There are commercial home alert systems that allow calls for help, including the always-stylish panic button worn as a necklace or bracelet and set up to automatically summon help through a 24-hour call center.

You may have aging eyes. A fascinating body of research suggests that many of the problems associated with aging (memory loss, slower reaction time, insomnia, and even depression), are possibly caused by *aging eyes* that filter out blue light. Does the home have bright indoor lighting? Skylights? LED light bulbs?

Frayed and overloaded wiring causes fires. This gets boring for us too. We know a frayed joke.

> *A bar refused to serve strings. So a thirsty string tied itself into a knot and entered. The bartender asked, "Are you a string?"*
>
> *"No, I'm frayed not."*

Structural changes may be needed (wheelchair ramps, widened hallways, modified bathroom facilities). Landlords *must* allow these changes as long as it is agreed they will be removed when you move out.

An occupational therapist can be quite helpful in making specific suggestions. For example, if the person is a gardener but has knee or hip problems, raised plant beds can work wonders. Someone with bad arthritis will find level door handles more friendly than doorknobs.

Guns. Having a gun in the house makes many feel much safer. However, grandchildren are anxious to play cops and robbers. And there's suicide. Depression and anxiety can come on fast. Maybe you don't want a gun around.

Opioids. If you have painkillers, keep them where teens can't get them—they can become regular killers.

Pets. Pets should stay even if they're trouble. They can be really important to quality of life. If you don't have a pet, consider getting one. Dogs are best, according to age researchers. They provide not only walks but companionship. Not that there is anything wrong with cats.

New devices such as Amazon's Alexa hold great promise. You talk to them, they talk back and keep track of things.

Alexa, remind me to take my medicine.

Alexa, read me a mystery.

Alexa, play "Hey Jude."

Alexa, phone Jane.

And, of course,

Alexa, find me friends, engross me in activities, and make me happy.

6

Assisted Living

*Tell your children how lucky they are that
you're considering this.*

There are marvelous places for Dad (and maybe you). Swimming pools, writing groups, Bible study groups, field trips, rides to shopping and doctors, even pickleball. And good food and new friends, folks who remember where they were when Kennedy was assassinated; new friends who were coaches, pilots, chefs, nurses, teachers, homemakers, and reporters; folks with different interests and experiences; and folks from different towns, states, and countries. None with nose rings. Way cool.

But there is a downside. It's a strain meeting people, smiling at people, people who have traveled the world, kayaked the Nile, who have broken bread with presidents, authors, and your favorite movie stars, people whose son has become a tenured professor at Harvard and whose daughter is a brain surgeon at Johns Hopkins, people who in the last election voted for that idiot. (Gore Vidal once said, "Every time a friend succeeds I die a little.")

A lot can be said for solitude and the Walter Mitty life you've led. Maybe a "senior community" is for you. Check them out. Much less expensive, licensed, with a family atmosphere, about ten or so residents, and shared meals, but no pickleball. Be sure to ask if they have 24-hour nursing care.

Your goal? A place to live that meets you and your spouse's interests and needs, not just in the next few months but the next few years.

It's a big decision, the biggest. Costs, location, care, activities. Shop around. You won't know why you like one unless you see others. There'll be greeters to show you around, sing the praises, and hope to close the deal. They're fine, but sneak off and talk to as many residents as you can. Go to lunch.

"What's the best thing about this place?"

"What's the worst?"

"What did you do today?"

"What's the food like?

"How's transport to shopping and doctors?"

"Do you play pickleball?"

Most facilities charge monthly; some require a large buy in. If the latter, be careful. Some have gone bankrupt.

Some things to find out from the administrator:

- Staff turnover—too frequent is not good.
- How are medical problems handled?
- What are the activities? How are complaints handled?
- How is it determined when someone should be moved to where they can get more assistance?
- How many people have moved out and for what reason?
- Do you enjoy working here?

Ask questions, start early, and don't rush.

Part Two

The Good News

7

Sex

Men spend more energy thinking and talking about
sex than on the act itself.

HARVARD MEDICAL SCHOOL

Sex is not dead. It's not even past. (Sorry Faulkner.)

Recalling going to drive-ins, but not the movies they saw, 90% of men and 70% of women continue to have sexual fantasies and many go, as we used to say, "All the way." There are senior dating services and even senior porn (or so we've been told).

Sex has many health benefits, from lowering blood pressure to helping keep your immune system humming. If you're not convinced, go to WebMD and read "10 Surprising Health Benefits of Sex." Celibacy can be a psychological and medical problem. Frank discussions between spouses, sex therapy, and talking with doctors can help.

Sexually transmitted diseases are hard to discuss with your doctor, but they are becoming more common. There are treatments, and things can get worse. As they say, be careful out there. Is sex exercise? Depends. It is, sort of, ranking between mild and moderate. Is it safe? Heart attacks during sex are very rare.

What about Viagra? It's fairly safe *except for men taking nitrate medications in any form.* For them it is very dangerous. (We're not doctors but do read the Harvard Medical School magazine.)

Sex, as always, is more than sex. It's intimacy with another, a source of emotional support, and a validation of self-worth. It might be simply caresses and gentle touching. Self-help manuals abound describing elder-friendly techniques. "*It's not your grand-kids' sex!*"

So what does the law have to say about sex?

Competent consenting adults, in privacy, can do what they want. Recently the Supreme Court underscored this right by striking down a Texas statute that criminalized gay sex, holding that it violated the Due Process Right of privacy.

Consent has limits. Violent sex is criminal, as is sex forced on a spouse. Spouses have the legal right to say "No"—it's still rape despite the fact they're married.

Consent obtained by threats, tricks, force, drugs, or booze is not consent. Nor is the "consent" given by someone legally unable to consent, children, and the mentally ill. *What about individuals with dementia?* Is their consent valid? If only a mildly cognitively impaired they can give consent, but if greatly cognitively impaired they can't; it's sexual assault.

If there is no valid consent the perpetrator is guilty of a crime and, in addition to prison, can be sued for money damages. So too can anyone who has a duty to protect the victim. Retirement facilities face a problem. Some rat out non-married consenters to their family, while others, realizing the therapeutic good flowing from relationships, openly discuss geriatric sex.

In 1952 Sandra Day O'Connor graduated third in her Stanford Law class. When she applied at law firms they thought she was applying to be a secretary. Now a law school is named after her at Arizona State University. Times change.

She retired from the United States Supreme Court to help care for her husband who was suffering from dementia and living in a continuing care facility. She discovered that he had fallen in love with another patient and, realizing his happiness, she willingly stepped aside. In 2018, she announced that she too had dementia and retired from public life. So it goes.

Love isn't dead, it's not even past.

8

Grandkids

*Grandchildren don't stay young forever, which is good,
Pop-pops have only so many horsey rides in them.*

GENE PETTET

Warning: If you have guns or pain meds around make sure your grandkids can't get at them. They are, in the words of the law, an "attractive nuisance."

Your grandchildren are growing up in a much different world than you or even your children did. IPhones, computers, Facebook, drugs, active shooter drills, and, of course, lousy music.

On a positive note, movies, TV shows, and commercials now feature interracial and LGBTQ couples. Even eating habits are changing. To protect their health and help the environment many are giving up red meat, and it is thought that about 10% of millennials are vegetarian or vegan.

This means your grandchildren will have different attitudes, interests, and probably values than you have, just like you had different attitudes, interests, and values than your grandparents, who never appreciated the genius of Pink Floyd.

Of course many things stay the same. Children still need a place to come home to, an occasional sit-down dinner, and grandparents who listen as well as lecture.

In addition to trips to Disneyland, occasional babysitting, and the impossible task of figuring out what they want for their birthday, you may want to set aside money for your grandchildren's education or, if they have a disability, help provide for their life expenses. We'll tell you how and then turn to the more difficult task of actually raising them. And give you a few answers about what happens if the parents die, if they won't let you visit, or if they are neglecting the kids.

COLLEGE FUNDS

Back in the day most colleges were essentially free. No more. Many cannot afford to go to college, and those who can are likely to graduate with a large debt, often over $100,000. That debt will mean they can't pursue their life dream of curing cancer, teaching in the inner city, or writing books for seniors, but must instead take a job with Phillip Morris.

Start a 529 Education Account. The money you contribute will grow tax free if it is used for education. While your *contributions* aren't deductible for federal tax purposes many states allow them to be deducted for state income taxes.

Talk to your bank about opening a 529 account. There are many choices and some restrictions. See www.savingforcollege .com.

HELPING DISABLED GRANDCHILDREN

You'll have to set up a "special needs trust" so that money you give will not just offset any other welfare or disability monies the child receives. That's a real danger. Your lawyer can explain this.

RAISING GRANDCHILDREN

It won't be a walk in the park. Probably bad things have happened; their parents have died or have fallen victim to drugs. After this heartbreak, the children walk into a new family and new home.

You're not alone. There are 2.5 million families in your position. There are local support groups and your Area Council on Aging can help. So too can Generations United (www.gu.org) and the AARP's Grandparent Information Center (www.aarp.org). There's also a new federal program, Support for Grandparents Raising Grandchildren, that will collect and distribute information for grandparents.

Legal Problems. Physical custody is not *legal* custody—doctors, dentists, and principals may require *parental* consent. For *temporary stays*, say over the summer or until the parents can relocate, the parents should notify doctors and school officials. Many states permit a short-term (usually six months or a year) designation of someone to act on behalf of a parent—the document might be called a "power of attorney" and statutory forms are often available. A "to it may concern" letter should help as well (notarized is best: bells and whistles always impress the reluctant).

If things look permanent, consider a *guardianship* or *adoption*. Without one you and the child are subject to the whim of the parent suddenly reappearing years later to take the child. Some states have "permanent guardianships."

Finances. Social Security benefits may be available for grandchildren. Children of retirees, including adoptive children, under 18 (or disabled), may be entitled to benefits. So too grandchildren being raised by a grandparent who dies or becomes disabled.

Local welfare offices and Area Council on Aging might have good tips on finding needed support. There is also abundant information (in a searchable format) on Social Security benefits available on the www.ssa.gov website.

Finally, a few questions we hope you'll never need answered.

What happens if their parents die?

When a parent dies, the survivor automatically assumes legal and physical custody of the child even if there was a divorce that gave custody to the other parent. If both parents die, the state probate court will appoint a guardian for the child and usually, but not always, the court will follow the wishes of the parents expressed in their will. But the court will always try to do what's in the best interests of the child.

What if parents won't let me visit?

Most states have laws that allow judges to order grandparent visitations over the objections of the parents. These are very limited, as much discretion is given the parent. Counselors are better at this than lawyers.

What if they're abused or neglected?

Report your fears to Child Protective Services. They will investigate. The reports are confidential. If your fears are confirmed, there will be a court hearing with the state as the moving party. The judge may order counseling in the hopes of keeping the family together or remove the children temporally to live with other relatives or foster parents while the parents work out their problems. In extreme cases parental rights may be severed and the children put up for adoption.

9

Remarriage and Divorce

Remarriage, the triumph of hope over experience.

We stole the line from Samuel Johnson. He'd be pleased. We'll start with remarriage; the joyous, wonderful event itself, your friends making funny toasts, mothers and fathers either sad or relieved. Then the rest of the story. All the things that can go wrong. We're lawyers.

First, your kids might not be too happy if you remarry.

The idea that their fathers and mothers should marry and enjoy themselves is always a thing horrible to be thought of in the minds of the rising generation.

So wrote Anthony Trollope 150 years ago. Things don't change. Trollope was a contemporary of Charles Dickens and thought by some to be the better writer. If you're into old English novels, give him a try; start with *The Warden*.

Remarriage requires busy work.

1. Rewrite wills and trusts.
2. Review IRA beneficiary designations, life insurance, and property and bank accounts held in joint ownership and notify Social Security.

Rewriting legal documents every five years is a good idea: "*You mean I was leaving money to that worthless jerk who said that about me last Thanksgiving?*" Rewriting them at time of remarriage is essential; otherwise fights are certain down the road.

There's a special problem if one or both of the happy couple have children. Usually newlyweds rewrite their wills, leaving their estate to their surviving spouse and, at his or her death, with the reminder of the estate going to the children. But not to put too fine a point on it, you'll be dead. How can be sure your new spouse (now grieving spouse) will keep the bargain and not write a new will and leave your money to his or her kids? Betrayal! Shakespearean tragedy!

A *living trust*, a marvelous device for many reasons, solves this problem. All the property goes in the trust for joint use during their lifetimes; when one dies, the trust becomes *irrevocable*, with the estate going to support the survivor and then, at the death of the survivor, the remainder goes to kids.

Consider a *prenuptial*, which is a written agreement between the happy couple hedging their bets. It's difficult to tell dearly beloved you want a prenup. Blame it on us.

It can cover such things as:

1. Who is responsible for the debts brought into the marriage?

2. In the event of divorce, what happens to the property brought into the marriage and to property acquired during it? What of support obligations?

3. Who is to inherit what?

4. Who takes out the garbage and who does the laundry?

Four isn't a joke (at least not much of one). We all get set in our ways. Marriages require adjustments. It might be well to hammer some things out—such as vacations, hobbies, relationships with adult children, and things of that ilk. These concerns may seem petty, but they are the stuff of life.

If one of you watches Fox and the other MSNBC, reconsider.

To make a prenuptial legally enforceable, as there is the potential for overreaching and misunderstanding, *each person* should be represented by separate lawyers. *Full disclosure* of assets and debts must be made; otherwise, a court will throw it out.

DIVORCE

"I promised to be with you in health and sickness, in good times and in bad times, but not 24 hours a day."

Retirement triggers problems. Daily routines must be renegotiated and long suppressed emotional problems, often having nothing to do with the marriage, may suddenly poison relationships. For example, some Vietnam veterans are showing up in PTSD clinics; horrible memories, suppressed for years, come rushing back when they retire.

Divorce is usually a disaster. Counseling, or separate bedrooms, may be better choices. From a legal standpoint, a divorce makes sense in two situations, neither of which is to "get even." The two: when one wants to remarry or when one needs governmental assistance under programs such as Medicaid (but if that's the goal consult a lawyer specializing in Medicaid planning—the rules are very confusing).

Why a disaster? Lawyers put it this way:

"Representing murderers I represent bad people at their best, representing divorce clients I represent good people at their worst."

Most states have "no fault" divorces allowing the couple to split if they have "irreconcilable differences"; adultery is no longer required. Along with forcing private detectives to sell their cameras, no fault divorce, some argue, has reduced marriage to something like a long date. Fortunately, that's beyond our scope.

As to *property* distribution, state laws differ, some following the old Spanish tradition of *community property*, others the English tradition of *dower or individual ownership*. While there are nice theoretical distinctions between the two, as a practical matter most judges (and state divorce laws) will try to equally *divide* the property acquired during a long-term marriage. This is easier said than done. Houses, pensions, paintings, oriental rugs, cats, and dogs are hard to value. You'll need lawyers.

If one of the parties is the breadwinner, there will be the matter of *alimony*, now called *spousal maintenance*. The basic notion is to "maintain" the non-working (or less-earning) spouse at relatively the same standard of living. But good luck for either party to live at their previous standard.

What about health insurance? If one spouse is covered by the other's policy, divorce will likely end that coverage or dramatically increase its cost.

Finally, unlike face creams and teeth whiteners, divorce doesn't make you any younger.

Separate bedrooms. No need to divide property, to obtain additional health insurance, or to pay a lawyer.

One way to avoid all of the problems of divorce is to avoid a marriage; just have a long date. Live together. Like our kids. But there may be "palimony." Lee Marvin, the star of *Cat Bellou*, was sued by his long-time live-in girlfriend for something like alimony. He made out better in the gun fight.

Part Three

Slings and Arrows

10

Strokes, Bad Meds, Hearing Loss, and Opioids

A dusty saloon, a kicked over poker table, a piano in the corner, cowboys backing away, and two old codgers reaching for their six-shooters.

"Slim, what did you call me?"

"I called you a liar."

"Oh that's OK. I thought you called me a lawyer."

That doesn't really fit, but so what. Lawyer jokes always work.

STROKES

FAST: Face Arms Speech Time

Common signs of stroke: face and arms go numb and speech becomes slurred. Time is critical. If medical help arrives quickly (in less than three hours), long-term damage can often be avoided. Err on the side of caution. Strokes are common, know *FAST*.

Lowering high blood pressure can *dramatically* reduce your risk of stroke according to the UC Berkeley Health and Wellness Alerts. You may not know you have high blood pressure. Your first sign might be instant death. It's known as the "silent killer." It's usually controllable by diet, exercise, and meds.

INSOMNIA

Half of us toss and turn and curse our fate. It's serious, causing falls, confusion, depression, car wrecks, compromised immune systems, and unpleasantness at breakfast.

Sleeping pills should be the last choice. People who routinely take them are nearly five times as likely to die over a two-and-a-half year period. Even though this study overestimates the risk (folks who routinely take sleeping pills probably are sicker than those who don't), there is little doubt that sleeping pills can adversely affect memory and coordination.

It's best to try other remedies: no caffeine or exercise three hours before bed, gentle activities an hour before (yoga, stretching, slow and deep breathing), and a bedtime routine.

We take naps. There are two problems with naps: sleeping too long and waking up groggy. Kenney drinks a cup of coffee and sets the alarm for 20 minutes. It takes the caffeine about 20 minutes to kick in, and he's good to go. Larry just sets the alarm for 30 minutes, and he is good to go . . . sort of.

Rather than tossing and turning, make the best of a bad situation; get up and read a while. Reading law books works wonders.

BAD MEDS

Many of us take the wrong dosage or the wrong drugs, which is more likely if we have more than one doctor. Doctors *don't talk* with each other (a major problem with our health care system). Drugs they prescribe may interact badly. Pharmacists can help by reviewing a list of all the meds, *including over the counter medications* and *vitamins*.

Check for side effects. Some meds lead to insomnia and others to depression. And don't tell your doctors to prescribe some drug you saw on TV—docs know better, and there are usually cheaper options; they went to med school, not ad school.

HEARING LOSS

"How's that?" Hearing loss ruins lives. It leads to isolation, may accelerate dementia, and, because the ear plays a role in balance, may lead to falls. If you or a loved one has a hearing loss and you haven't corrected it, shame on you.

Vast improvements have been made in hearing devices both in terms of quality and price. While traditional hearing aids cost over $4,000, new devices, sold online and at retail stores, often go for $300 to $500. They do not require an exam by an audiologist but they are effective for mild to moderate hearing loss.

Hearing aids are not covered by Medicare but some medical insurance policies do cover the cost, as do some Medicare Advantage plans. You can get information on state and federal financial help from the Better Hearing Institute (1-800-Ear-Well). Hear Now (1-800-648-HEAR or 303-695-7797 hearing impaired).

"Hearing loops" hold great promise. Installed in public buildings and theaters they transmit words and music directly to a hearing aid: no background noise. Local initiatives, supported by the Hearing Loss Association of America and the American Academy of Audiology, hope to make them common.

WHISKEY RIVER RUNS DRY

Sorry, Willie, it should. We can't drink like we used to. We need no testimonials. Red wine? It's pushed as a good thing for heart disease. But not too much. The National Institute of Alcohol Abuse and Alcoholism recommends no more than one drink a day.

The Whiskey River hasn't run dry for everyone. Many sink into the pit of alcoholism. There are many good programs like AA that often work. But getting the abuser into treatment is hard. An "intervention" might work. Friends and family confront the person, not with "you're harming yourself," but with "you're making things horrible for us."

Smoking? Everyone plans to quit after the next big event in their lives. But hey, there is always a big event looming. The ICU is the ultimate big event.

OPIOIDS

Many are addicted and many are dying. We only have a few things to say. If pain meds are prescribed:

1. Lock them up! Teenage grandchildren, bless their hearts, steal them from medicine cabinets to get high.
2. Don't take more than prescribed even if pain continues. Run out and you'll end up buying heroin on the street.
3. Don't believe a little hit never hurt—it leads to addiction and ruined lives.

Narcan can save lives in the case of overdose by reversing respiratory depression. If someone you know is addicted talk to your druggist—no prescription is needed.

11

Scams and Identity Theft

My kids are in jail in Mexico and need money,
my Social Security was suspended, but the good news an
African prince will send me $1million.

You can fool some of the people some of the time—and
that's enough to make a decent living.

W.C. FIELDS

Fooled? Cheated? You're in good company, with all those smug, overachieving Harvard Business School grads who fell for Bernie Madoff's promise of 20% returns.

As you read this there are very smart people out there *plotting*. We'll warn you of some of the common frauds and recount the delightful story of the Holland Furnace Company. But first, if you have been cheated, do something.

Call a lawyer helpline; most local Bar Associations have them. Your county attorney's office can also help, and police can point you in the right direction.

Lawsuits are possible if you've been cheated by a company. State laws prohibit consumer fraud and may give you the right to get your money back and sue for damages. Your attorney fees may be paid by whoever defrauded you. *Small claims court* is another possibility. Easy forms, no need for a lawyer, just tell the judge what happened. You can even sue a large corporation there, and usually they can't bring their lawyers.

If you've been cheated a little amount by a large corporation you might become the lead plaintiff in a million dollar class action. See a lawyer; there are those that specialize. (Without class actions big players could cheat little players and get away with it.)

IDENTITY THEFT

Thieves get account numbers (Social Security, credit card, bank), open accounts, run up bills, and don't pay them, unless they're very new to the game. They go through mailboxes and garbage, invade computers, work in offices that have numbers, and some even get numbers the old fashioned way: stealing wallets and purses.

Alert from Chase Bank Security. Third parties have attempted to access your account. We will have to suspend your access to your accounts, unless you send us, immediately, your Social Security number, your account and PIN numbers, your date of birth, your mother's maiden name, and your favorite flavor of ice cream.

This is known as *"phishing."* The bait comes in many forms: "alerts," "updates for your credit union," "unauthorized activity warnings," "immediate cancellation of your trading privileges." The emails look quite official and some purport to be from the U.S. government.

Never trust unsolicited emails, letters, or phone calls. No bank, financial institution, or governmental agency, *will ever request that you send financial information.* (Crooks will.)

Don't keep your Social Security card in your purse or wallet. Some routine forms (doctor offices, department stores) have blanks for Social Security numbers; leave them blank. Buy a crisscross shredder and use it. If you're not sure, shred it. Keep important documents (tax records) in locked files. Identity thieves may be relatives, colleagues, visitors, or, we kid you not, plumbers!

The Federal Trade Commission's identity theft hotline is 1-877-438-4338.

There are companies offering insurance against identity theft, but we don't know much about them. You're on your own.

SCAMS

It's fairly easy to hang up on robo calls—try it, you'll like it—but we were raised to be polite, so it's harder to get rid of real people. Learn to hang up.

"Sorry, I can't talk right now. Give me your number and I'll call you back."

Even better, just hang up. Trust us. Your robo caller won't take it personally. Get on the National Do Not Call Registry: http://www.donotcall.gov/1-888-382-1222, TTY 1-866-290-4236. Use your phone to block all unknown callers.

Don't answer unless you know who is calling. If they're legitimate, they'll leave a voicemail message. If your landline doesn't have an answering machine, buy one; it's well worth one avoided scam.

Probably the most dangerous scam is the *health care scam*; it costs you money and endangers your health. Fraudulent cures cost money, delay cure, and kill. No matter the ailment, from cancer to wrinkles, from alcoholism to ulcers, someone is selling a miracle cure. Just say no.

The American Medical Association advises extreme caution if the cure is claimed to be quick and easy or that it involves a "secret" formula or machine to cure disease.

Alas, you haven't won $50,000 in the Canadian lottery and to get your winnings simply send back $200 to cover expenses. By the way, your chances of winning a lottery are the same whether you play or not, but we digress.

Clever schemers, fearing that they might have to get a real job, have come up with something new: *a relative* or *friend in trouble*. A call from a granddaughter who needs $500 immediately or she will spend the night in some horrible jail. Or an email from a friend claiming to be in Europe without funds because he was robbed. These contacts may seem legitimate—scammers can get a lot personal information from Facebook.

Home Mortgage Scams. Crooks offer loans (door-to-door, by mail, or through the internet) allowing you to pay off bills and requiring only low monthly payments. Lower payments do not necessarily mean lower interest; they mean a longer time paying back the loan. Or you may be offered an extremely low rate. These schemers aren't interested in collecting your monthly payment. They are interested in getting your house by foreclosure.

Never take on a mortgage from a company you haven't heard of or haven't checked out.

Home Repair Scams. Someone claiming to be a city inspector shows up to check your house for violations. Forget it. He isn't with the city. Tom Hanks, or his double, offers a *free* roof or furnace inspection.

Dollars to donuts the home will need repairs. And, oh yes, you will need to pay them before they can make the repair. If you think they might be legit, ask them to come back in a week. If they are, they will.

Finally, the long-awaited Holland Furnace Company story. They offered a free furnace inspection, tore it apart, and then offered to put it back together for several hundred dollars. As luck would have it, one day it was the Godfather's furnace.

There are happy endings even in the world of scams.

12

Driving

I want to die like my grandfather, quietly in my sleep.
Not like his passengers, screaming in the back seat.

Funny line, but children do get run over by aging drivers.

Drivers over 75 have more fatal accidents than any other age group save teenagers. Elderly drivers are 7.5 times more likely to crash, exceeding the rate of even drunk drivers. Why? Slower reactions, heart attacks, impaired vision—particularly night vision—and dementia

One hopeful note. Cars are getting so much safer the driver is becoming somewhat irrelevant.

New devices are making cars almost self-driving. They brake, steer, and warn of cars in your blind spot and of cars approaching from the side. And they can wake up granddad if he is drifting off the highway.

But they don't do much about left turns.

Before buying a new car with all the safety stuff ask yourself if you need a car at all. Shopping is now so easy with Amazon rushing to you everything from toilet paper to the complete works of Shakespeare, and Lyft and Uber standing by to take you to the movies. Car trips? Rent yourself a Lincoln; your neighborhood street will suddenly transform into a beautiful curved forest road and you into a movie star.

Okay, you won't stop driving.

STAYING ALIVE

The AARP offers a driver refresher course (the Smart Driver Course, formerly called 55 Alive). Commercial driving schools offer programs as well. While these courses certainly cannot hurt, and may help individual drivers, there is (sadly) little evidence that the functional driving abilities lost with normal aging can be compensated for by training, even specialized training.

Certain medications can affect driving ability. Check with the doctor or pharmacist. *Avoid rush hour, left turns, night driving, and frequent trips.* Co-pilots help.

Convincing Granddad to stop. Understand his resentment. Cars are more than transportation. Our first driver's license meant drive-ins, McDonald's, and *Happy Days.* Giving it up signals a loss of independence, vitality, and control. Bummer.

Family doctors might help, and many states require a driving test for elders. Private evaluators are available. Call the MVD for advice. Simply suspending the license will not stop every driver. Plates can be removed, keys hidden, and spark plugs disconnected.

Legal warnings help.

- If you run over someone, you may be changed with vehicle manslaughter and spend your golden years in prison.
- You will be sued for damages. If judgment against you exceeds your insurance coverage, the person you injured can come after your life savings. It is no defense that you didn't mean to do it or that you'll have to go on welfare.

Bad idea to loan granddad your car. The injured party may come after you on the theory you were at fault for loaning him the car.

Moral warnings do better.

"Do you want your last memory to be of the child you ran over?"

13

Age Discrimination

"Sorry to let you go, old goat."

In our next chapter we deal with discrimination against goats. Here we discuss age discrimination.

Mandatory retirement was outlawed when Congress passed the Age Discrimination in Employment Act (ADEA), with narrow exceptions for matters of public safety, for example, airline pilots. It protects people 40 and older from discrimination in terms of hiring, firing, promotion, and pay. It applies to part-time and temporary workers as well.

This law applies to almost all employers (private and public, profit and non-profit) but only if the employer has *20 or more employees*. Some states have laws that protect those who work for smaller employers.

Employers can fire for bad job performances, even if those poor performances are due to the aging process Employers can reduce the work force, as long as they do not single out the elderly. But they can't simply assume that the older workers can't do the job even if some cannot. Individual decisions must be made.

It is a violation of law to have a *job requirement* that is not really needed if it acts to discriminate against the elderly. They can't insist that you are able to lift 50 pounds if your job never requires you to do that.

Seniors facing adverse job action on the job based on age may have a claim under federal law and maybe even under state law. If that sounds like you, contact an employment attorney.

Because older employees tend to use their health care insurance more, to avoid higher insurance premiums a company might refuse to hire or might fire (or force into retirement, or make life hell so that they quit) older workers. This is against the law. See a lawyer and sue away.

14

Disability Discrimination

A disability is bad enough. People ignore you or treat you as a child, talk really slowly, mouthing their words. If you're hassled at work or in finding a place to live you may have a legal claim.

A few quick points. While we focus on federal law, many states have parallel anti-discrimination laws which may provide for broader relief ("more money"). Most are enforced by governmental agencies. It is easy to report discrimination and let them investigate. But you need to act quickly or the statute of limitations will prevent you from suing or getting any relief—money.

DISABILITY DISCRIMINATION IN EMPLOYMENT

The federal law, Americans with Disabilities Act (ADA), protects disabled individuals in employment. An employer must make *"reasonable accommodations for known physical or mental limitations of an otherwise qualified individual."*

For example, your employer may be required to help you do your job by changing the height of your desk, providing additional training, or offering more frequent rest breaks. Employers with fewer than 15 regular workers are exempt from this federal protection, but the state may have a law that applies to employers with fewer employees.

Disabled individuals may also face discrimination in government programs (no programs for the deaf in school) and in public accommodations and facilities (no ramps in retail stores). If you face discrimination because of a disability, contact the federal Equal Employment Opportunities Commission (EEOC), which enforces the ADA, or the state's Attorney General's Office.

DISABILITY DISCRIMINATION IN HOUSING

Under the ADA it is illegal to refuse to *rent or sell* to persons because they are disabled. An individual is disabled if they have a "physical or mental impairment that substantially limits" one of the major life activities, such as walking, unless the handicap would threaten the health and safety of others or would lead to substantial destruction of property.

The only housing exempted from the ADA are single dwelling residences rented or sold without a Realtor; small housing complexes of four or fewer units where the owner occupies one; and housing run by religious organizations and private clubs.

It is also a violation of federal law to refuse to rent or sell to a tenant because of race, color, religion, sex, or national origin. Those protections are provided by the Civil Rights Act of 1964.

An important note to renters with a disability. You may have the right, at your expense, to make *reasonable modifications* (for example, to put in ramps or grab bars, or lower or raise counters) to accommodate the handicap if you agree to restore the place to its original condition when you leave.

If you are a victim of housing discrimination contact the federal Department of Housing and Urban Development (HUD) or a state housing enforcement agency.

DISCRIMINATION AGAINST ANIMALS

Assistance or therapy animals must be accommodated in nearly all housing, not just government-subsidized housing. Someone with a recognized disability is entitled to keep an assistance or therapy animal in rental units. No formal training is required to make your dog or cat an assistance or therapy animal. Emotional support is one of the services such an animal can provide.

As to *pets*, owners of *federally assisted housing*, designated for the elderly or disabled, cannot have flat rules against pets. The landlord can only prohibit pets that are a nuisance or a threat to the health or safety of others.

Friendly dogs, cats, and goldfish are fine but no lions, crocodiles, or T-Rex.

15

Elder Abuse and Neglect

All happy families are alike; each unhappy family is unhappy in its own way.
LEO TOLSTOY

Bad things happen on Boardwalk as well as Baltic Avenue.

We'll first talk about physical abuse or neglect, then financial exploitation, and, to remind you there are still some good things, we'll close with a wonderful poem by Edna St. Vincent Millay, if we can figure out how to make it fit.

Jane and John have always been a loving couple.

Don't be misled by smiling Polaroid pictures. Loving couples may find it hard to cope with retirement. In a sense it's a whole different relationship. Old conflicts may come back.

Too much free time and too little money can undermine a relationship.

IF YOU SUSPECT ABUSE OR NEGLECT

Stay in touch. If you haven't heard from a loved one in some time, call or, better yet, visit. Abusers keep their victims isolated.

"Jane's a little too tired to come to the phone just now." Or "She isn't up to seeing visitors." If you don't hear from them, *they don't hear from you.* Think how horrible it must be to be abused or neglected and not hear from loved ones.

Don't dismiss *complaints* as grumpiness or discount bruises, burns, welts, cuts, punctures, sprains, broken bones, dehydration, weight loss, missing eyeglasses, hearing aids, or dentures. Abusers will explain these away as the results of falls or illnesses. Insist on details.

Insomnia, excessive sleep, and change in appetite may indicate depression and hopelessness due to *psychological abuse.* So too can tearfulness, paranoia, low self-esteem, excessive fears, ambivalence, confusion, resignation, or agitation.

Other signs of abuse come, not from the victim, but from the *caregiver.* Is the caregiver drinking? Depressed? Resentful? Overworked? Or, alas, driving a new car?

Victims often blame themselves, thinking they deserve it, and some believe that being abused shows that they can no longer run their lives, that they are getting senile.

- *"I'm concerned that someone may be mistreating you. I know this is very hard for you to talk about. It's not your fault. I won't think less of you no matter what you tell me."*
- *"You may fear what's going to happen to you if your caregiver gets into trouble. There are ways to protect you and get you someone else to care for you."*
- *"Abuse gets worse, not better. Even if the person has promised never to do it again."*

WHAT CAN YOU DO?

Consider the caregiver. Often abuse is triggered by overwork; the solution may be respite care or additional help. Help is also available for alcohol and drug abuse. We have a chapter on caregiving that you might find helpful.

Maybe you should have a good talk with the caregiver, pointing out that police and prosecutors are beginning to target elder abuse and that these aren't defenses:

- the victim was hard to deal with
- the victim abused me in the past

But in most cases preventing abuse is best left to the experts. Human relationships are always complicated. Abuse is not always a one-way street, not always a black and white affair. Some victims trigger abuse by being too demanding, too sarcastic, too unappreciative. There may be payoffs for the victim, a sense of vindication when the abuser strikes out, and then, on bended knee and with flowers, seeks forgiveness.

Adult Protective Services are the folks to contact (if not the police). The national clearing house: 1-800-677-1116.

Although state laws differ, often doctors and medical professionals, social and welfare workers, and even bankers, accountants, and lawyers may be *required* to report if they know of or suspect physical abuse, neglect, or financial exploitation. Even if you're not required to report abuse, do the right thing—report it.

ABUSE BY FAMILY MEMBERS: PROTECTIVE ORDERS

In most states a battered spouse (it's not always the wife) can go to court, fill out a simple form, and get an order requiring the aggressor to stay away, even if it means moving out of the house. No need for a lawyer. If the abuser shows up anyway they can be arrested for violating the order; they need *not* do anything more in terms of threats or abuse.

MENTALLY IMPAIRED VICTIMS

An emergency *guardianship* can remove the victim from an abusive situation. An emergency *conservatorship* can freeze assets to protect against financial exploitation.

CIVIL COMMITMENT

Under most state laws, mentally ill individuals who present a danger to themselves (not eating, threatening suicide) or to others (not careful with fire), can be taken into emergency custody and, after a hearing, committed to a mental hospital for treatment. The length of the commitment and the procedures vary according to state statute. Contact Adult Protective Services.

FINANCIAL ABUSE

If you suspect *financial* abuse, take a look at the victim's bank account. Be alert for checks to the caregiver or cash withdrawals. Look at credit card statements and examine the purchases and amount owed. Look for the sudden inability to pay bills, withdrawals of large amounts of cash, and living well below their means. Children steal ("Well, I'll get the money later, anyway"); paid caregivers steal ("Well, I should be paid better"). Get background checks on home-care workers—they may not be what they seem to be.

Others exploit the elderly in less criminal ways, often targeting those who live alone: *home shopping channels* target the lonely, *charities* guilt trip the victim, *political action* committees offer protection from the other party, and door-to-door salesmen offer new roofs.

FLYING OFF TO VEGAS: SELF ABUSE

If a loved one begins to waste money or is frequently off to Vegas, a guardianship or, in some states, a conservatorship can be sought on an emergency basis. The appointed guardian or conservator will take charge of the person's finances—bank accounts, property, stocks, and the like. Before that, banks, credit card companies, and financial institutions can be notified.

The rub: what looks like reckless may be sowing one's oats. Say an aging aunt is taking the gardener on weekend trips to Vegas.

Unless she no longer has legal capacity or unless he is putting undue pressure on her, she is free to spend her money any way she wants to get what she wants—fun—even if it means you won't get what you want—money.

Finally, Edna St. Vincent Millay:

My candle burns at both ends;
It will not last the night;
But ah, my foes, and oh, my friends—
It gives a lovely light!

Part Four

~

Slowing Down Time's Winged Chariot

16

Memory Pills, Supplements, and Diets

People taking Super Pill are happy.

Pill X is 100% more effective that Pill Y.

We're not doctors and don't even play them on TV. But we know a thing or two because we've seen a thing or two. (Sorry.)

A quick review. Learn new things to keep your mind engaged, check your blood pressure to keep heart pumping, and make your house safe to keep you walking.

In thinking about pills, mistakes can be made.

People taking Super Pill are happy.

Did you run out and buy Super Pill? But does Super Pill *cause* happiness? Or is there simply a *correlation*—people taking Super Pill happen to be happy but Super Pill has nothing to do with it.

Pill X is 100% more effective that Pill Y in curing Condition Z.

Wow, buy Pill X. But wait. If Pill Y cures only one in a hundred cases of Condition Z while Pill X cures two, that's a 100% improvement, but it's not worth rushing to the drug store. Be leery of percentage claims.

Who to trust? Doctors and pharmacists know best. There is good information on the Web on neutral sites (e.g., WebMD). As to TV ads, those smiling people, playing with adorable kids, who are now free of a disease you never heard of and didn't know you had, those folks aren't real patients, they play them on TV. They get paid; no wonder they're smiling.

SUPPLEMENTS

Many are a waste of money; they do no good and possibly do harm. Prescription drugs must pass three tests.

Phase One: Are they toxic?

Phase Two: Are they better than a placebo?

Phase Three: What's the proper dosage?

These tests can cost hundreds of thousands of dollars and involve hundreds of people. To prevent results being skewed by the placebo effect *double blind procedures* are used, where neither the doctor nor the patient know if the drug is a placebo or the drug being evaluated.

Supplements are not subject to any of these tests. Listen carefully to the ads. At the end, the announcer may admit that none of the claims have been authenticated. A supplement may or may not be good for you, but your buying of it is certainly good for whoever sells it.

"Natural" doesn't mean better: think poisonous mushrooms. Very organic, very natural, very deadly.

For certain conditions supplements are needed. But take your doctor's or pharmacist's word, not your aunt's.

DRUGS TO IMPROVE MEMORY

At our age they're popular. About 25% of folks over 50 take something to improve brain health with the promise of enhanced memory and sharper attention and focus. The problem? There's no solid proof any of them work, and there's no federal regulation or testing of the claims made by those who sell them.

But what about the jelly fish? There was, and perhaps still is, an ad for a supplement that claimed to improve memory by relying on a compound found in jelly fish. Okay, but do jelly fish have good memories? We looked into it . . . at least we think we did. "Larry?"

Doing the daily crossword puzzle is good for you . . . if being better at crosswords appeals to you. As for improving your brain, not so much.

The market is flooded with computer games claiming to make you smarter by selling you mind-bender puzzles and assuring you that if you solve them, you'll stay mentally in shape. There is no solid evidence they work, but they are fun, and, at our age, it's a thrill to be told you're getting better at something.

DIETS

Being overweight can cause health problems. Of course there is considerable debate over when a person is overweight. We all gain weight as we age; don't lament each pound. But if you want to shed a few pounds be of good cheer. You can lose weight at any age.

Seldom does a TV program go by without a diet commercial, evidence that most don't work. Sure, they may help you lose weight, but you'll probably gain it again—and more.

Instead change your diet. No more fast food, large servings, and third glasses of wine, even if they are red. We'll not bore you with the virtues of fruit, vegetables, and the Mediterranean diet except to underscore that processed foods and sugary foods are bad and that folks who eat less red meat have less heart disease (cause or correlation?) and they help the environment—raising cows and pigs makes huge demands on the environment (in more ways than you think).

Exercise is wonderful, but it won't help much to lose weight. Do 30 hard, sweaty minutes on the stationary bike, and you'll find you worked off one cookie, and a small one at that.

SLEEP

Sleep, perchance to dream, ay, there's the rub, what dreams may come? At 2 in the morning who cares?

Over-the-counter sleep pills can cause problems if used too often and even some prescribed pills, which worked for a younger you, may now be terrible. Think Ambien.

17

Exercise

Let no potbelly evade your eyes, Exercise!

Whenever I get the urge to exercise
I lie down until it passes.

MARK TWAIN

You know you should, but, like most of us, you don't or you don't do enough—whatever enough might be. You know you should get off the couch. Here are some ideas that might help.

As we get a bit older we need to engage in three kinds of exercise.

1. Aerobic: like running, swimming, walking, or fleeing from zombies.
2. Strength: like weightlifting, resistance training, or breaking rocks with a sledgehammer.
3. Stretching: like yoga . . . you know, stretching.

Aerobics keeps your heart in shape, lowers your blood pressure and cholesterol, and burns calories.

Strength exercising helps your muscles to be strong enough to do the things you want to do, and also helps reduce the risk of osteoporosis and the symptoms of arthritis, heart disease, and type 2 diabetes.

Stretching is good for your joints and will keep you more flexible, limber, and energized, while it improves your balance and your looks.

How to get from "should" to "would"?

Decide that exercise is not just something you should do, but like brushing your teeth, is something you do regularly. Set aside a regular time every day that you exercise. Feel guilty if you don't. Pat your belly.

Consider joining a health club. Some Medicare Advantage plans and employer provided health care insurance offer the Silver Slippers program that pays the fees.

Maybe a personal trainer is right for you. Sure it's expensive, but what's more important, feeling good or that new outfit? Once or twice a week sessions with a trainer will mean you will actually exercise regularly. You also will learn how to exercise in ways that are best for you. If you can afford a trainer, it's worth it.

Get a smart phone like an iPhone and listen to it while you work out. Exercise is much easier and goes faster if you're listening to NPR, novels, and, especially, music. We are partial to classic rock: "Smoke on the water, fire in the sky."

If not an iPhone, get a friend. Many of us prefer companionship when we exercise. Better to talk to a friend than stare at the wall. Exercising with others has even more benefits. The best is that you have to show up for your exercise. It's a funny thing about we humans, we like to fulfill our promises. If I agree to join a group of six others at 8:00 a.m. to walk through the park, I'll most likely show up. Even if it is a bit gloomy outside or I am feeling pretty tired, I'll make it.

You will also exercise better with friends. You jog that extra half-mile because you don't want the others to see you quit. When your weight training partner suggests you move up to the 10-pound weights, you'll give a try. And honestly, who does yoga alone?

We don't want to hear your excuses for why you don't exercise. We have used the same excuses.

I'm too out of shape. Who isn't?

I'm too busy. Come on, even ten minutes can work wonders.

It's too painful, it hurts! Start slow.

Start with the 2-pound weights rather than the 5 pounders. Walk one lap around the track this week. Next week try for two. Embarrassed at how poorly you do the downward-facing dog in yoga class? Get over it. No one cares about your form. They're too busy worrying about their own.

In possible violation of a trademark, we're going to say, *Just Do It.* Get out there and do something. Whatever you do is better than doing nothing. Can't get yourself to do a daily 30 minute walk? Research shows that three daily walks of 10 minutes each are just about as good for you. Not ready for the weight room? Buy some light weights and use them while watching TV. Yoga is not for you? Find a good stretching video on YouTube and do it while listening to some favorite tunes.

Keep in mind. Those who do the daily **A**(erobics), **S**(trength training), and **S**(tretching) will have a better looking one. (Sorry.)

18

Dealing with Doctors

"Now, what I want you to do, right when you get home, and this is very important, is to qubt twri pzcv jmottm plbtk!"

DOC MARTIN

You'll feign understanding, not wanting to look stupid, not wanting to seem like you're "losing it." Studies have confirmed that many patients leave their doctor's office without understanding the advice or, even worse, getting it wrong. (Studies have also confirmed that the sun sets in the West, but they caution that past performance is no guarantee of future performance.)

Our advice: *Repeat their advice!*

Repeat their advice!

This assures you get it right, helps you remember it, and fills in gaps: "Should I take those pills together?"

TAKE AUNT MOLLY

When it comes to the discussion of diagnosis and treatment, it is good to have someone there to recall the information and to occasionally act as your advocate.

BEING HEARD

In criminal court a defendant complains, "Your Honor,
I want a new lawyer. This one never pays any attention to me."
The judge asks, "What about that, Counselor?"
"Sorry, Your Honor, I wasn't paying attention."

Professionals aren't good listeners. Doctors interrupt their patients in the first *18 seconds* of the visit. (Yep, there was a study that proves this.) As for lawyers, rather than listening to you, they want to hear what they have to say.

This is not good. Both doctors and lawyers quickly conclude what the problem is, and then ask questions to confirm and solve it. But unless they listen they may get the wrong problem. One doctor advises others, "If you listen to your patients they are telling you the diagnosis."

PREPARING

Take a list of your medications, including over-the-counter ones, because they may trigger bad interactions, may render proscribed medications worthless, or are worthless.

A prioritized list of concerns helps; the real one, the embarrassing one, shouldn't be the last one you raise on the way out the door.

"Oh, one other thing, I have, or maybe I have, you know, like erectile dysfunction." (Thanks to the power of advertising this is no longer embarrassing, indeed, it is on the cusp becoming a badge of masculinity.)

As to internet research, there are some good sites which can sharpen questions and make the most of the doctor's advice.

But beware of TV ads suggesting ills you didn't know you had and telling you of the medicine you didn't know you needed. The drugs they push may not be right and are probably more expensive than those that are just as effective.

ERRORS PATIENTS MAKE

Don't ignore *weight loss*. It can point to a serious illness. *Sleep loss* should also be brought up. It can be treated.

Another common error is to generalize from specific instances. *"Cousin Mel had the same condition, and he took Brand X and got better. Give me Brand X."*

But maybe Cousin Mel didn't have the same condition; maybe he would have gotten better without Brand X; maybe he came within an inch of suicide.

ERRORS DOCTORS MAKE

It's flu season. You wake up with the classic signs: fever, cough, aches and pains. What do you conclude? Flu. You're not alone. Probably your doctor would too. "A lot of that is going around." Both of you might be *wrong*.

In a terrific book, *How Doctors Think*, Dr. Jerome Groopman warns that doctors often misdiagnose, perhaps 1 out of 10 times. Like the rest of us, they jump to conclusions. To make sure they haven't, Dr. Groopman recommends we ask three questions:

1. *What else could it be?* ("Well now that you mention it, it could be . . .")

2. *Is there anything in the exam or tests that doesn't fit?* ("Well, now that you mention it, your fever isn't typical.")

3. *Is it possible I have more than one problem?* ("Well, now that you mention it, sometimes folks get the flu because they are already sick with . . .")

A good friend, Dr. Jack Boyer, suggests a few others:

4. *Have you considered whether I want to get the treatment or not?* (Maybe you'll live with the condition rather than taking more drugs and risking side effects.)

5. *How long will it be before I get the medical tests back? Should I call? Do you have a portal where I can go and check myself?*

Another good friend, Dr. Scott Bronnimann, adds:

6. *If I'm not getting better how long should I wait before calling?*

Doctors don't like giving bad news, and patients don't like hearing it. However it is essential.

7. *Would it surprise you if I die within the next few months?*

19

Dealing with Surgeons

Minor surgery is when they do it to someone else.

BILL WALTON

Surgery is serious. We'll give you some things to think about and what to do when you leave the hospital. But when you arrive at the hospital, after the insurance questions, after the HIPAA paper (don't ask), and signing a pile of papers drafted with great precision by hordes of lawyers but never read by anyone, you might be asked if you want a DNR.

A DNR? Do Not Resuscitate. You've seen *Code Blue* on TV where all the gorgeous nurses and cute doctors run past crying family members to a prostrate patient and shout, "Stand back" and zap the patient and everyone lives happily ever after. A DNR tells them to forget it and continue with their flirting.

Why would you not want one? Because zapping is painful, breaks ribs, and often doesn't work. If it does keep you alive, you will probably only live for a week or so. Talk to the medical staff about your odds; they're worse than you hoped.

Next question, do you want the surgery?

You can say "no," even if it means you will die. If you are not conscious or lack enough mental capacity, the decision will be made by doctors and family. That's another chapter. Let's assume you are making the decision.

Your doctor tells you the surgery is a good idea, but is it? He's trained to save lives and never to give up. Dr. Pauline Chen, a professor at UCLA, writes of texts given to medical students. They outline the series of steps to take in dealing with an illness.

Medicine presumes physical action. On no branch of the decision tree, however, is there a box reserved for Do nothing or Hold tight or Sit on your hands.

The surgeon might over-evaluate the benefits and under-evaluate the risks. *Do the opposite.* Are there alternatives? How long is the rehab? How many have had the surgery and lived? What are the dangers of the many pain meds that you will be given before and after the procedure?

Here are the $64 questions:

"What will my life be like if I have the surgery?"
"What if I don't?"

Near the end of life many opt for surgery in hopes of a medical miracle. Be cautious. Think hospice. A study of almost two million Medicare patients found that nearly *one in three* had surgery the last year of life, *one in five* in the last month, and *one in ten* in the last week.

Second opinions are mandatory.

HOSPITALIZATION

You survive. Hospital stays are getting shorter. You may be too weak or frail to go home so you might be transferred to a care facility for a week or two. If you are on Medicare you might want to check to see if it pays. Home care is another Medicare option.

Coming home you'll need support. There's an alarming rate of readmission, frequently with problems other than the original one. A relative or friend should insist on understanding what needs to be done to prevent relapse. Often this will involve several medications and several doctors.

"Was that two pills every hour or one pill every two hours?"

So you don't survive. Is that so bad? A friend was in a bad accident. During the procedure the surgeon remarked, "I think we can save him."

"Funny," he recalled, "I remember thinking it would be okay if they saved my life but it would be fine if I died."

In *The Brothers Karamazov* an old man reflects,

The grief, by a great mystery of human life, gradually passes into quiet, tender joy; instead of the young, ebullient bloods comes a mild, serene old age; I bless the sun's rising each day and my heart sings as before, but now I love the setting even more, its long slanting rays, and with them, mild, tender memories, dear images for the whole of a long and blessed life.

20

Dealing with Lawyers

*In good times lawyers are great jokes,
in bad, great friends.*

*You need a pour over trust with the
children taking per stirpes.*

*When was the last time your computer
offered you coffee?*

Lawyers, like doctors, talk jargon (give them a break, they spent many sleepless nights learning it). Like dealing with doctors, repeat their advice to make sure you understand it. Ask questions. Don't go alone. Take Uncle Bob; you took Aunt Mollie with you to Doc Martin.

Taking Uncle Bob presents a couple of problems. First, with him in the room what you tell the lawyer is not confidential. But alas, at our age we have very few confidential matters; few of us are drug dealers seeking income tax advice or philanderers seeking a divorce.

That what you say isn't confidential means the lawyer can tell others, like your spouse or adult children, what you told him.

However, if you are discussing your will and want to leave Bob something, he can't be in the room even if you want him there. Your lawyer wants to be sure giving Bob money is your idea, not his.

So why not stay at home and open your computer? Sure, you'll save money. But take a look at our chapters on estate planning. There are bewildering number of options, all with pros and cons: wills, trusts, trusts for special needs, joint ownership, lifetime giving, health care powers of attorney, living wills, and living trusts.

But let's assume you know exactly what you want. You tell your computer, and it tells you how to do it. Simple, but not so good. Good lawyers, before they tell you how to do it, make sure you really want it. They'll ask questions. They may also offer you coffee.

"Have you considered other options?"

"How will you feel about what you decide today in a couple of months? In a couple of years?"

"How will your decision affect your family, your friends, your community next week now and in the years to come?"

And, of course,

"Do you realize all the things that can go wrong? I do."

Computers don't chat. Talking to your lawyer you might have a few questions about finding a good retirement facility or about the tax implications of selling your house. Your lawyer will even have answers for questions that you didn't know you should ask. This isn't their first rodeo.

There are lawyers who specialize in elder law. In fact, there is a national organization, the National Academy of Elder Law Attorneys. It has a terrific website with scads of information and will provide a list of lawyers in your area. Your local bar association can also give your names of lawyers by area of practice.

Other than their bills, clients resent most that lawyers seldom give clear "yes or no" answers. But that's because the law seldom gives "yes or no" answers. A famous book for law students is *Getting to Maybe*. Oliver Wendell Holmes, a towering Supreme

Court Justice, and a Union soldier in the Civil War, responded to the notion that the law must be certain to give repose.

Certainty is illusion and repose is not the destiny of man.

Yeah, we've noticed.

Part Five

Money and Health Woes

21

Reverse Mortgages and Selling or Renting Your House

Anyone living within their means suffers from a lack of imagination.

OSCAR WILDE

For most of us our house is our major asset. If you decide to move you can sell it, rent it, or give it to your kids. We'll look at these choices. If you are staying put and need cash, you can borrow against it. Get a home equity loan or take out a reverse mortgage.

SELLING YOUR HOUSE: THE TAX MAN

If you get too cold, I'll tax the heat, if you take a walk, I'll tax your feet, I'm the Tax Man

George Harrison knew rhymes. We'll try. "*Sell for more than you paid, I'll tax what you made.*"

If you paid $100,000 for your house and are selling it for $500,000, congratulations. You have made a *capital gain*, and that may be taxable by the feds. Here the amount gained is $400,000. But the Taxman, always a good sport, will ignore $250,000 if you're single and $500,000 if you're married. That means, if you're single, you only have a capital gain of $150,000 and, if you're married, tequila!

There are certain restrictions on these exemptions dealing with how long you've lived in the house and how long you've owned it. For most of us those restrictions shouldn't be a problem, but check. Also some states impose capital gain taxes.

GIVING YOUR HOUSE TO THE KIDS

If you plan to give your kids the family home *don't do it* just yet. If you give it to them in your will, they'll get a *stepped up basis*, the amount it was worth when you died, here $500,000. However, if you give it to them as a lifetime gift they get your original basis ($100,000) and because they don't live in it, if they sell for $500,000, they'll have a $400,000 capital gain.

RENTING YOUR HOUSE

Being a landlord is worse than sitting through a tax class. There are professional services to do it for you. But if you insist on doing it yourself and enjoy getting up in the middle of the night to fix a toilet, check with your accountant as to what you can deduct from your rental income.

STAYING PUT AND GETTING CASH: REVERSE MORTGAGES

If you're short of cash, check with your bank about a home equity loan. You're old enough to know how these work, so let's look at the new kid on the block, reverse mortgages.

Considering a reserve mortgage? To learn all about the federally insured Home Equity Conversion Mortgage or HECM see:

https://www.hud.gov/program_offices/housing/sfh/hecm/hecmhome

Here are the basics. On television, aging actors (time hasn't been any kinder to them, even with their makeup) assure you of the wonders of reverse mortgages, where the bank loans *you* money. You can stay living in your house, go to Hawaii, pay off large credit card loans, or simply kick back and watch *Happy Days* reruns. It's a 30-second spot so they can't mention interest, closing costs, and related fees (or maybe time hasn't been that kind to their memories).

You don't have to make monthly payments. The loan only falls due when you die, move, or fail to keep the place up. If it is not repaid then the bank will foreclose, sell the house, and take the first bite. Of course your heirs can repay the loan or work something out with the bank.

You must be at least age 62. If you and your spouse own a house jointly and one of you is not 62, the one of you who is 62 or older can take out the mortgage on their own. You can terminate the loan early.

There is good news. Because the money you get is a loan, it's not taxed, and it won't affect your right to Social Security. You continue to own your house and can continue to live there. There are no income limits on who can take out a reverse mortgage. Any kind of house can qualify, from mansion to house trailer. But cooperative apartments, most second homes, and newly built homes, less than a year old, do not qualify.

The loan can be taken as a lump-sum, such as $50,000. But more likely you'll use the loan of $50,000 as a line of credit. Because you're paying interest, it's better to take out the money over time rather than all at once.

You take out money as you need it. For example, maybe you take out $15,000 to buy a car. Later you borrow $7,000 to pay off your credit cards. Another way is to arrange for the lender to send you a check every month to give you more spending money. For example, you arrange to get $200 a month until you reach the $50,000 limit.

If you're getting the loan to go Hawaii or pay someone's tuition, congrats. If you're borrowing to pay off a large medical bill, see a lawyer about *bankruptcy*. Your local bar association can give you names, and most lawyers give free consultations or charge very little.

And one more bit of advice, avoid payday or title loans like the plague.

22

Social Security

The only thing we have to fear is
Social Security going broke.

Social Security is the child of the Great Depression, folks selling apples, losing farms, and Franklin Roosevelt on the radio assuring the nation, *"The only thing we have to fear is Fear itself."*

It has been a tremendous success.

- The poverty rate among folks over 65 is no longer 70%, as it was before Social Security; it is now 12%.
- More than 42 million retirees currently receive retirement benefits, as do millions of families of workers who died or became disabled.
- For over half of Social Security retirees, the program provides the majority of their income.
- Its administrative costs are about 1%, compared to around 15% for private pension plans.

If the program collapses, the needs of seniors will be shifted to sons and daughters, welfare programs, and soup lines. So it's not likely to be allowed to collapse.

The basic framework is that you pay Social Security taxes on your earnings up to about $138,000. It's the FICA box on your paycheck.

There is a lot of talk about it going broke as our population ages. Young folks pay in, and old folks take out. That worked wonderfully for decades, but now we old codgers are hanging on longer, and there are fewer young workers to pay in.

To save the program, some (those earning less than $138,000) say taxes should be paid well beyond $138,000. Folks with cushy jobs, like professors, think it would be fine to raise the retirement age to 70. Another solution is to let in more young migrants.

But this isn't a book about politics. Let's move on.

Who's eligible and when?

Eligibility. You have to work and pay into the system for 40 quarters. If that is all you work, your benefits will be small but *you'll be eligible for Medicare* (otherwise it costs a bundle). The more quarters you work, the greater your benefits. It is possible to be eligible for benefits even with a shorter work history if you become disabled and can't work.

EARLY, LATE, AND FULL RETIREMENT

At "full retirement age" you receive your full retirement amount, called the "Primary Insurance Amount." Full retirement age is slowly going up; for folks born in 1954 or later, it goes up two months every year until for those born after 1959 full retirement age will be 67.

Early Retirement. At 62 (that age is not going up, though the percentage reduction from normal retirement benefits is) you can retire and collect your Social Security benefits. Should you? The answer is—it depends.

There are a host of factors to consider, such as your health and other sources of income. Three things you must know.

First. You won't be eligible for Medicare until 65 even if you claim your Social Security benefits at a younger age. If you retire before age 65, you can continue your employer's health insurance but must pay the premium.

Second. If you continue working, and you have not reached your full retirement age, after about $18,000 of earnings, your Social Security benefit will be reduced $1 for every $2 earned.

Third. If you claim benefits at age 62, you will have a permanent reduction of 25% to 30% in monthly benefits from what you would have gotten if you waited until your full retirement age.

Some private pension plans have what is known as an integration of benefits clause that reduces your pension payments in light of what you receive from Social Security. Depending on the rate of reduction, it might be wise to delay taking Social Security as long as possible.

Late retirement. If you wait to claim benefits until you are 70, your check may be as much as 32% higher (and you are still eligible for Medicare at 65). After the age of 70, there is no further increase in benefits.

TAXES ON BENEFITS

If your income is over a threshold amount (currently about $25,000 for a single taxpayer or $32,000 for a married couple) up to 50% of your Social Security payments will be counted as income. (It's 85% if you're in the highest 1% of income earners.) You can request Social Security to withhold federal taxes for you. However, it cannot withhold state taxes.

How does Social Security compute your benefits? Like this:

A train leaves New York going west at 70 mph. Two hours and 13 minutes later, another train leaves Los Angeles, going east at 68 mph. What is the capital of Nova Scotia?

Well not exactly, but you get the point.

Suffice to say, the longer you work and the higher your earnings, the more your benefit. The average benefit is around $1,400. For a comfortable retirement folks need about 70% or 80% of pre-retirement income. It's a *serious mistake* to think that Social Security will maintain your standard of living.

The system favors lower end earners. Workers who have earned half the national average will receive about 56% of their average salary, average earning workers about 42%, while folks at the high end typically get about 28%.

INSURANCE BENEFITS

Social Security is more than a retirement program. If an insured worker becomes permanently disabled *disability* benefits are available. Benefits are also paid to survivors upon the death of a covered worker.

FAMILY BENEFITS

Family members might receive benefits. This includes spouses, children, and even dependent grandchildren and dependent parents. It's worth a call to Social Security. Divorcees who were married at least ten years and have not remarried before age 60 are entitled to a benefit equal to (usually) one-half of the retiree's retirement amount. The divorcee's benefits are usually available at their age 62, or younger if they are providing care for a dependent minor.

23

Pensions

*When we were youngsters Moms made the small decisions,
like what to have for dinner, what house to buy, and where
the kids should go to college, and Dads made the big
decisions, like who to root for in the Rose Bowl.*

Times change, even the Rose Bowl is no longer a big deal. However in many families one spouse handles the finances, leaving the other in the dark. Before getting into the weeds, the other should be brought up to speed—dementia or death are possible. Community colleges may have courses; so too the AARP.

Now the weeds.

BASIC PLANS

Defined Benefit Plans. These pay a pension that is based on a percentage of earnings (usually the average of the last three to five years). The percentage, say 2% per year, is multiplied by the number of years worked. If you worked 30 years, your pension is 60% of your average earnings over the last few years. The pension is taxed as regular income by the feds.

Defined Contribution Plans. The employer and perhaps the employee make contributions to a retirement account that is invested. When you retire, you usually get the amount of money in the account as your retirement benefit.

401(k) Plans. Similar to defined contribution plans, but they give the employee somewhat more flexibility as to how much to contribute. The employer may match an employee's contributions up to a certain amount.

How much money you will have in your 401(k) plans depends a lot on how much you and your employer put into the account and how successfully you invest the account while you are working.

CONTRIBUTIONS AND VESTING

You are entitled to get back all of your contribution no matter if you are laid off, fired, or quit. However, you are not be entitled to the employer's contributions until they vest. Most vest after five years, but this varies widely: some vest in a month, some in seven years (the maximum length under federal tax law).

Some employers fire folks shortly before their retirement rights vest or, in the alternative, make their jobs so miserable that they quit, known as a "constructive discharge." If this happened to you, get in touch with an employment lawyer. You may have legal recourse.

DECISIONS AT RETIREMENT:
CASHING OUT AND ANNUITIES

If you have a pension coming, you may be given the choice to reject the pension and instead take a large, lump-sum payment.

If you take the lump sum, it will be taxed as current income. Ouch! You can avoid that by rolling over the lump sum into an IRA. Thereafter, you will be taxed only on the amounts you take out of the IRA.

If you accept the pension, you will get a lifetime annuity. You will get a monthly check until both you and your spouse have died unless both of you have agreed that the pension should stop when you die. If you elect that option, the monthly check will be larger, but when you die your spouse will not get any more money. Usually that is not the way to go.

PENSION TROUBLES

Divorce. The worth of the pension usually will have to be divided—and this gets complicated. Don't worry, your ex-spouse's lawyer will know how this works.

Forgotten pensions. They're like the Chance Card: "Bank Error in Your Favor." If you worked for the ABC Co. back in the day, they may owe you a pension. Track them down. Old tax forms will give the employer's tax number and perhaps the number of the retirement plan. For a fee, the IRS will provide a copy. With these numbers, perhaps the Pension Benefit Guaranty Corporation can help (1-800-400-PBGC). www.pbgc.gov.

IRAS

Because the money that was paid into your 401(k) was a deduction from your income, it is taxed as income when it is withdrawn. The money earned on the account or in the IRA to which you rolled over the 401(k) money is not taxed until it is withdrawn. This is why IRAs are generally the last cookie jar that you dip your hand into. It's better to first withdraw from saving accounts.

However, beginning in the year after you turn 72, there are annual required minimum distributions (RMDs) from the IRA.

Roth IRAs are better than a regular IRA when it comes time to get money out. First, there is no need to take any out for the owner's lifetime. Second, all the money you take out of it (after it has been around for five years, that is), *including* the amount it earned, is tax free. This is because the money you put into the Roth IRA was not deductible at the time.

It is possible to convert a regular IRA into a Roth IRA. This may make sense although it will trigger a big tax bill.

As to how to invest the money in your IRA, buy low and sell high. Want some help? Look for a professional financial planner who is paid on a set or hourly fee.

24

Medicare

A, E, I, O, U, and sometimes Y

Working difficult puzzles makes you smarter. A hidden benefit of Medicare. But don't curse your fate: Medicare is wonderful.

It provides medical insurance to over 60 million Americans. You can sign up (and you should) when you turn 65 and are *eligible* for Social Security. You need not be drawing your benefits. You're eligible for Social Security if you've worked and paid in for at least 10 years or are married to someone who is eligible.

You may get Medicare before 65 if you are disabled or have end-stage renal disease—kidney failure.

Because it is a governmental program, it can be confusing. First of all, there are four parts, called imaginatively, Part A, Part B, Part C, and Part D.

Part A is hospital insurance. It pays for most costs of being in a hospital.

Part B pays your doctors for 80% of what they charge, leaving you to pay 20%.

Part C gives you the option of enrolling in a Medicare Advantage Plan instead of Parts A and B. (We warned you this could get confusing.) You get everything that Parts A and B provide, and MORE. How much more depends on the plan you enroll in.

Part D pays for some of the cost of your prescription drugs—note that it pays for *prescription* drugs, not for those over the counter (a big cost for many seniors) or for "recreational" drugs.

If you are turning age 65, you need to learn a lot about Medicare, or you can just run off and join the French Foreign Legion. You have many choices to make. So get online, go to meetings offered by your employer, and buy books that devote pages and pages to explaining Medicare. Even better go to Medicare.gov, which is a great, free source of information.

All we are going to do is give you some basics.

Medicare Part A is free. You don't pay anything—you already have paid for years because of the Medicare wage tax that was deducted from your earnings.

When you turn age 65, enroll in Medicare Part A even if you are still working and even if you have other health care insurance. For how to enroll go to Medicare.gov. If you are collecting Social Security benefits, you will be automatically enrolled.

Medicare Part B pays for 80% of doctor visits, some outpatient care, and for most durable medical equipment like a wheelchair. It also pays for outpatient mental health care.

Unlike butterflies, Part B is not free. You pay a monthly premium based on your income. It's about $135/month (in 2020); it goes up if you're Bill Gates.

Part B is a good deal. Private insurance with the same coverage would cost more. If you are collecting Social Security, the premium is deducted from your monthly benefit payment.

You will have to pay a Part B deductible of $198 (in 2020) and the remaining 20% of the doctor's bill.

We know what some of you are thinking. "I won't take on Part B and the cost of the premium until I'm sick and need it." Sorry, but Uncle Sam thought you might try that. So if you wait, the premium gets higher and higher each year.

Part C. Way too complicated. We'll come back to it.

Part D. You pay a monthly premium. You enroll in a Part D (prescription drugs) when you retire. There are many, many Part D plans. Get ready to spend some time figuring out what plan is right for you. Later, when you realize you enrolled in the wrong plan, *don't panic*, you can change your plan every year.

Back to Part C. Medicare Advantage Plans. You can choose an Advantage Plan instead of enrolling in Parts A, B, and D. When you turn 65 and most years after that, your mailbox will be stuffed with ads for Medicare Advantage Plans. For unbiased information go the government's Medicare website.

Here is the quick overview of Medicare Advantage Plans. They provide all the benefits that Part A and Part B provide plus additional benefits that might include prescription drug coverage, dental benefits, and vision benefits. Advantage Plans also usually don't have co-pays and deductibles like Medicare Parts A and B.

You give up some choice in who your medical providers are in return for more benefits. The plan will limit which doctors that you can see and may limit what hospitals it will pay for.

About one third of Medicare beneficiaries are enrolled in a Medicare Advantage Plan. Check out the plans offered where you live. You may decide that it is the smart choice—or you may prefer to not have a limited list of doctors and hospitals to choose from.

If you don't enroll in a Medicare Advantage Plan, you need to look into buying a *Medicare Supplement Plan* that is sold by a private insurance company to pay for what Medicare Part A and Part B don't pay for. There are about a dozen different kinds of plans that are labeled, you guessed it, A, B, C and so on. They all have the same coverage no matter which insurance company offers it, but prices vary. So, as the old song has it, "You Better Shop Around."

Confused? Things could be worse. You could have to pay for all the cost of your medical care.

Part Six

Mental Illness

25

Senior Moments and Dementia

When we were young and forgot why we walked into a room, we would shrug and look around. Now it's "Oh no, early Alzheimer's!"

We all fear Alzheimer's even if we can't spell it. However we've been having senior moments since childhood. It takes a little time for short-term memories to be stored. People who have been knocked out will not remember what happened right before; they lose consciousness before the memory could be stored. Say you tell yourself "I will go into that room to make the bed." Ha. When you get there the phone rings and that memory of your intentions is knocked out.

What about forgetting names? There is something known as "crowdedness." We have more stuff in our minds to sort through to find the dentist's name. In grade school, with three friends, we were spot on.

That said there is a slight decrease in short-term memory after the age 30. Not to worry, at least not too much. Odds are you won't develop dementia.

What are the odds? The National Institute on Aging estimates that 5% of those 65 to 74 suffer from dementia. After age 85, 50% have some degree of dementia.

Forgetting big things, missing appointments, and getting lost are signs of dementia.

The first thing is to know how terrifying it is to be forgetting more and more each day, and losing control of your life. Read Lisa Genova's *Still Alice* or rent the movie.

Family members often have a very hard time. Putting aside the emotional anguish of helplessly watching the descent, there are practical problems that must be faced:

- Getting an evaluation
- Getting help
- Executing the needed documents
- Stopping the individual from driving
- Dealing with wandering off
- Considering alternative housing

GETTING HELP

Start with the Alzheimer's Association. Staffed by wonderful and knowledgeable people, it can provide valuable information and set you up with a local support group. 1-800-272-3900 (hearing impaired 312-335-8882).

We highly recommend *The 36-Hour Day* by Nancy L. Mace and Dr. Peter V. Rabins. It contains valuable advice, information, and comfort for anyone with a family member suffering from dementia. And there are blogs, such as Alzheimer's Reading Room.

If the patient is on Medicare, look into the possibility of home care, which is essentially free.

PUSH EARLY EVALUATION

There will be a lot of denial: "It was the holidays, no wonder she forgot all her appointments." "I think I had the flu. I'm fine."

The longer you put things off the worse it will become. Memory loss is often caused by correctable conditions: bad medicine interactions, alcohol, drugs, depression, hearing loss, and diabetes. While dementia cannot be cured, there are drugs to control some symptoms, and families can set in place procedures to deal more effectively with the individual's decline.

GET THE LEGAL DOCUMENTS
IN ORDER

This is a priority. The individual must have *legal capacity* to sign documents. Can the person recognize alternatives, weigh pros and cons, and project into the future? If so, they likely have legal capacity.

Make sure that they have the basic three documents: a *will, financial power of attorney,* and a *health care power of attorney.* Don't rely on the forms that clutter the Internet. Remember, you get what you pay for. Talk to a lawyer who can answer your questions and draft the documents that fit you and your family.

If you don't act soon an expensive and problematic guardianship may be required.

WANDERING OFF

This is a constant fear. If the individual has disappeared, call the police and tell them that the person has dementia (otherwise they won't take the matter seriously). The Safe Return Program can help. For a one-time registration fee, a bracelet and clothing tags will be provided with a toll-free number. If someone finds the person, they call the number and the operator will then contact the caregiver listed in the database. This service is available 24 hours a day.

Soon there will be shoes with transmitters embedded that will alert your phone if the person wanders off. Unlike bracelets and tags, these transmitters will not be removable. There is already an "app" for smartphones that will tell you as to where the individual is. For more information, call the Alzheimer's Association at 1-800-272-3900 (hearing impaired 312-335-8882).

DRIVING

Not knowing what room you're in is distressing; not knowing what street you're on is deadly.

No one wants to give up driving. In some cases, the family must take away and hide the car keys. But what about Tuesday's doctor appointment? Area Councils on Aging may have volunteer drivers or provide a professionally operated van. If the patient moves into assisted living, rides to shopping and doctors are usually included. And there's Uber and Lyft.

CONSIDERING ALTERNATIVE HOUSING

In the short term make sure your house is as safe as possible. In addition to the things we discussed in Chapter 5, "Making Your House Safe," make sure windows and doors are secure to prevent wandering and stairs made safe to prevent falls. Look in the bathroom and garage for things that might injure.

There will come a time, and with Alzheimer's it is almost a certainty, when home care is no longer an option. When is that time? When wandering off becomes routine, when the person hates one of the family, or when the caregiver is on the edge of physical violence.

Start looking for other living arrangements. There are many choices that offer various levels of support. Assisted care facilities can bridge the gap between independent living and nursing homes. Many offer different levels of care from apartment living to "special care units." There are also "adult foster homes" that have a family-like atmosphere. Some of them specialize in dementia care.

Then there are nursing homes. If they take Medicaid patients, and most do, they are licensed and inspected by the state. Usually about half of their residents live there because they have dementia.

There is no need to break the bank. All the person needs is a clean place to live, good food, and be stopped from wandering off. Senior living or assisted living facilities can often provide all the required support for someone with dementia who does not require extensive medical care. If the move to such a facility is made early, it may help delay or even prevent a move to a higher and more expensive level of care.

While Medicare does not cover long-term care, Medicaid, the program for the poor, does. If the person can't afford their cost of care, contact an elder law lawyer for advice as to how to qualify for Medicaid.

The one thing we leave you with:

No matter how hard it is for you, it's worse for them.

26

Depression

Granddad's gaining weight, drinking, not sleeping, can't make up his mind, has no interests, and has a short fuse.

Note the power of language:

Granddad is depressed.

Granddad has depression.

If we say "Granddad is depressed" our response is "Cheer up Pops" or "Damn it, knock it off." We've all been depressed, got over it, and moved on. We assume that depression isn't serious, is temporary, and is to a large degree in our control.

But if granddad has *depression*, it's a disease like cancer; it can't be willed away and needs treatment. He's not alone. About one in seven over 65 suffer depression and, of that number, 70% to 90% go untreated. It not only destroys their life but the lives of those around them. If you suspect depression, do something. Start with the family doctor.

> *"Granddad, you're not the same. You're depressed. It's an illness, like cancer, it's not your fault or in your control. You can get help. I've made an appointment with your doctor."*
>
> *"Mind your own business. I'm fine."*
>
> *"Granddad, it's my business. We love you. We want you to be well."*

Treatment works for 80% of those who seek it. There are new antidepressants and new treatments. Electric shock, the villain in *One Flew Over the Cuckoo's Nest*, is making a comeback. Some even say small doses of LSD, taken under proper supervision, help. Moving to San Francisco and giving peace a chance probably doesn't.

"None of drugs work. Waste of time."

"Granddad, the treatments take time to work. Remember how long it took you to teach me to ride a bike?"

We've come across some things that might work.

Walking. There is a link between physical and mental health. One study had severely depressed individuals walk on a treadmill for 30 minutes for ten days. They reported significant improvement.

Hanging out. We're social animals. Senior centers, clubs, bocce ball—anything to get out of the house. But not at the corner bar. Alcohol is a bad mix with depression.

Helping out. To overcome the sense of worthlessness, assign tasks. Walk the dog, rake the leaves, or take out the garbage.

Observing. Putting some distance between yourself and your illness might do wonders. If you find yourself in a funk, step back and ask, "Why am I depressed? What triggered it? What worked last time?"

Make plans and promises. Make a list, it can be a short one, of things you'll do today and promise yourself you will do them, even if you change your mind. Send a text to an old high school friend, go for a walk, or find a better program on Netflix.

Make your bed. That's the advice of Admiral William H. McRavena, a four-star admiral who headed the Seals. If you start your day with an accomplishment, it will instill a small sense of pride and will encourage you to do another task. Little things matter.

This strikes us as a terrific idea—someday we'll get around to trying it.

The good news is that mental illness is becoming seen as a disease, not a personality fault. If you've been to your free "Welcome to Medicare" checkup, your doctor wasn't being nosey. Under the Affordable Care Act depression screening is part of the "Welcome to Medicare" annual visits.

27

Guardianships

Uncle Don is out chasing windmills, rushing where the brave dare not go, and investing all the family money into To Reach the Unreachable Star, Inc. Something must be done!

Guardianships or *conservatorships* are serious. The "ward" forfeits some or all of their adulthood in the sense that some or all of their right to make their own decisions is taken from them. When should it be considered?

- When the individual lacks the mental capacity to manage their finances.
- When the individual lacks the capacity to make health decisions and their health is suffering badly, because they refuse needed treatment or to move into a nursing home to get needed treatment.
- When a disabled individual is being abused.

This is boring stuff. Unless you are serious considering a guardianship there are better ways to spend your time. You'll need a lawyer anyway.

A friend or relative can file a guardianship petition. They should be reluctant to do so and should be aware of their own self-interest—that the guardianship will make things easier for them or will preserve money that they will eventually get. A person's interest more often distorts their judgment than corrupts their heart.

Bad decisions don't necessarily mean lack of capacity. If the person retains mental capacity, roughly the ability to see and weigh alternatives and project into the future, they have the right to do what they will: refuse life-saving treatment, buy a very expensive car, or get a nose ring.

Mental capacity is not an all-or-nothing thing. A person can lack the ability to manage finances but be perfectly competent to decide where to live and what medical treatment to have. Competency may be variable over *time* (seniors can be more alert in the morning than in the evening), *setting* (dressing up and going to the lawyer's office may temporarily improve the senior's ability to focus) and *topic* (some seniors may be able to give extensive histories and care directions for their cats but not be able to identify all of their grandchildren by name).

Even these categories are too broad. Some courts will narrow a guardianship still further, say over the person's stocks and bonds but not management of their Social Security check and day-to-day finances.

TERMINOLOGY

Some states use "guardian" to identify a court-appointed person who makes medical decisions and "conservator" as the name for one appointed to handle finances. Some states use "guardian" to mean both, and some use "conservator" to cover both. Some states use "guardian" for wards who are minors and "conservator" for adult wards. In other words, watch your words.

EXPENSES

In almost all cases a lawyer will be needed for the petitioner, and a physician will likely be required to submit an affidavit stating that the person has a medical cause for their mental incapacity. Thus the costs may be substantial. If the petition is granted, all the costs must be paid by the ward. In many states (but not all), the proposed ward will have to pay for a court investigator if one is appointed.

HEARING

The court hearing comes quickly, usually in a few weeks. (The system will respond even more quickly if it is an emergency.) The ward has the right to be present. Some judges will even go to the person's residence, such as nursing home, to conduct the hearing.

The individual has a right to an attorney (to resist the guardianship or to object to a particular person nominated to be the guardian) and, in some states, if the individual has not selected a lawyer, one will automatically be appointed and will be paid by the ward's estate (or, if the ward is indigent, by the court). In some states, before the hearing, the court will appoint a court visitor or investigator.

Routine guardianships are usually quick. A short court hearing will be held with the person seeking the guardianship, his lawyer, and the lawyer for the ward (usually court appointed) meeting to see if all is in order.

Contested guardianships are more like trials. They are contested if the individual insists they are mentally competent, if relatives are in a fight over ending life-sustaining treatment, or if there is a fight over who should be the guardian.

At the hearing, the judge (or in some states a jury, if requested by the proposed ward) first decides whether the individual has mental capacity. If so, everyone goes home. If the decision goes against the individual, two questions remain: what kind of guardian should be appointed (financial or personal and with what powers), and who should be the guardian?

WHO SHOULD BE THE GUARDIAN?

Usually it will be the petitioner. In the case of large or complicated financial estates, it might be a bank or trust company, or a private professional fiduciary. If no family member volunteers to serve, the guardian can be a social service agency, which will usually charge a fee.

Public guardians, employed by the state or county, are available in some states for individuals who have no one else. In most communities some individuals serve as paid, professional guardians. Check if they are licensed (some states require it) and if they are bonded. There is a national certification for professional fiduciaries; it may not be required, but it might provide some comfort to know that the guardian is familiar with best practices and national trends.

Typically, family members serve without charge (though that is not necessarily the case). Expenses (lawyers, accountants, travel) can be charged against the ward's estate. Institutional and professional guardians charge for their services, usually on an hourly fee basis or for a percentage of the estate assets.

Guardians are given a court document to show to banks, doctors, and others (usually called "letters of guardianship" or something similar) and will probably be required to report back to the court yearly or even more frequently.

Part Seven

Care Giving

28

Deciding for Others

I'm only thinking of him, in my body, it's well known,
there is not one selfish bone.
DON QUIXOTE'S NIECE, planning to lock him up.

Before you decide for others recite:

My interest in this will distort my judgment far oftener than
corrupt my heart.

Maybe the niece wasn't corrupt, locking up her uncle for her benefit, but her interest in the family money distorted her judgment so that she believed it would be in his. (Sorry, you'll have to see the musical. You'll thank us.)

As a guardian, trustee, parent, son, or daughter you'll have to make very hard decisions.

"This is Doctor Morris at Mercy Hospital. Your mother has been in a bad accident and is unconscious. Her chances would improve if we amputate her arm. Tell us what should we do."

Once she told you that she would rather die than lose an arm. What do you decide? You have three choices:

1. Decide what you would do if you were her.
2. Decide what is best for her.
3. Decide what she would do, even if it's stupid.

We'll discuss what the law says, what you can do to get ready to make tough decisions, and how to be sure your interest is not leading you astray (although we know in *your* body there is not *one* selfish bone).

THE LAW

Number One, doing what you would do is the wrong choice. You're deciding for her, not you. She's the captain of her own ship even if she runs it ashore.

If you know what Mom would want, go for it. But what would she decide? "Sure, Mom said she would rather die than have an amputation, but she wasn't facing the decision. Who knows what she would say now?"

If you have no idea what Mom would want, decide what would be best for her. The law likes to call this deciding based on her "best interests."

As for what are Mom's "best interests," we pass.

This discussion probably hasn't helped you in the slightest, but we're lawyers and lawyers love meaningless distinctions. We're not the ones going to the hospital.

GETTING READY TO MAKE TOUGH DECISIONS

This section will be helpful. Before you have to make financial decisions for another person, ask them if they want security or growth in their investments. Do they want you to spend their money on them so that they can live it up, or save money for their grandkids?

Before making healthcare decisions, spend some time with the person and talk to them about their wishes. What kind of life is acceptable? What if they develop dementia? Become terminally ill? The more you talk with them, the more confident and less guilty you will feel about the decisions you make for them.

MAKING GOOD DECISIONS

Your parents are thinking of their retirement dream and moving to a mountain cabin. But they would be far from emergency help, and dad has a heart condition. They've asked for your advice.

The decision will trigger *economic, psychological, and social ripples,* not only today, but in years to come. When giving advice, don't focus too narrowly.

- How will the decision affect your finances next year and five years from now?
- How will it affect your family and friends next year and five years from now?
- Next year and five years from now, will you think you made the right decision?

You have a dog in the fight. If your parents stay in the city, you won't have to worry as much or drive as far.

Make sure that you are telling them what is best for them — not for you. Explain, however, how their decision will affect you. They need to know. Always ask, *"What's my dog in this fight, and is it distorting my judgment?"*

29

Caring for Others

"In the unlikely event we experience severe turbulence," the smiling flight attendant warns, "the oxygen mask above your head will drop down and . . ."

At this point nervous flyers tune out and fail to hear, "If you have children with you put your mask on first."

Expect turbulence, severe turbulence. Grab the mask.

You're not alone in caring for another. In almost one in four homes someone is caring for a relative with a physical or mental disability. A typical caregiver spends about 18 hours a week providing care: doctor visits, managing finances, and hands-on help. Two-thirds work outside the home and, of these, more than half have to make workplace adjustments: coming in late, going part-time, giving up promotions.

There are scores of books, websites, and local groups, such as your Council on Aging, that can provide wonderful advice and assistance. For now, a brief overview of some legal and financial issues.

If you work, ask about flextime. Some employers have elder-care programs to help employees who are caregivers. Under the

Family and Medical Leave Act, companies with more than 50 employees must allow *unpaid* leave to care for sick family members. Some states allow for leaves with partial pay; in California it is six weeks at 55% of wages.

Working outside the home may make sense for your mental health even if you lose money, paying more for home care than you're earning. Getting out of the house is often therapeutic.

It's hard for your family to appreciate the costs of care. Siblings may accuse you of wasting money, of taking advantage, and, when the will is eventually read, of using undue influence to get more of the inheritance. Have a sit-down with the family early. Explain what you are up against. (Note: if the patient wants to make out a will in your favor, you must get a lawyer and you must leave the room when they meet.)

LAW STUFF

Get the patient to appoint you their agent under a health care power of attorney and sign an HIPAA release so you can discuss medical conditions with doctors.

If you'll be handling their finances, joint checking accounts will allow you to pay the bills. If the patient is receiving Social Security, contact the SSA to get advice. If dementia is an issue, you'll need a financial power of attorney. To play it safe get a lawyer to draft it and supervise the signing.

Handling money riggers temptations ("*It will be mine soon anyway*" and "*I'll borrow some now and pay it back later*"). Prosecutors aggressively pursue financial abuse of elders. Keeping records is essential not only to keep you clear of the law but also to prevent family fights.

FINANCIAL STUFF

Medicare does not pay for long-term home care, but some long-term insurance policies will.

If the patient is on Medicare and facing a terminal illness, definitely consider hospice. It offers home care, provides wonderful services, and allows the caregiver needed respite moments. See Chapter 39.

You may be entitled to a "dependent" deduction on your income taxes.

Individuals under 65 may qualify for Social Security Disability. The disability (disease, illness, condition) must be one that will last a year or result in death. That can include early-onset Alzheimer's.

Older folks may be entitled to many benefits: low cost drugs, food stamps, home care aides, and free transportation. The National Council on Aging has a slogan: "You Gave, Now Save!" Here are two information resources: Eldercare Locator 800-677-1116; www.eldercare.gov and www.benefitscheckup.org

PRACTICAL STUFF

Your well-being is critical. You'll need support, ideas, and time out. *Support groups*, organized around specific illnesses such as cancer, diabetes, heart disease, arthritis, or Alzheimer's, can be found at your local Area Council on Aging, or on the Web.

Adult day care can help. Book clubs, computer training, exercise, music, and art help those who attend to continue to lead a life, not just endure it. Folks do better with goals to pursue. A friend gives his mother a daily computer problem: "If I'm in London and want to go to Glasgow, what train would I take, how much would it cost, when would it leave, and do they serve tea?" She loves working on the problems.

Respite care, at the home or as temporary stays in a nursing home can be very helpful. Hiring part-time or full-time help is an option. The cost may be partly covered by insurance and Medicare. Geriatric care managers can help. While there is no licensing required, most come from the helping professions and are quite knowledgeable.

Updating family and friends, coordinating visits, and seeking help and advice can be made much easier by creating an email group or even a private website. Lotsa Helping Hands and Care-Zone can help. For individual calls, consider Skype or FaceTime.

Bottom line—*caring for another is very hard and you are at risk.* No doubt you will become fatigued and irritable. You might drink more, sleep less, and become abusive.

Remember what the flight attendant said.

30

Nursing Homes

They're better than in movies. Hollywood would have us stay young forever.

SELECTING A NURSING HOME

Some nursing homes are great; others, both figuratively and literally, stink. Remember, "It's location, location, location!"

Who to talk to? Hospital discharge planners, social workers, doctors, clergy, and volunteers who help the elderly. Every community has a long-term care ombudsman who visits nursing homes and takes complaints. They cannot recommend homes but can answer questions about complaints and survey results.

Visit at more than one and visit each several times, at different times of day. *Don't make appointments; just show up.*

Staffing. Is it adequate to give individual attention or overworked?

Mealtimes. Do residents socialize? Residents needing help should be integrated with other residents rather than eating alone.

Resident rooms. Personalized or institutionalized?

Residents. Reasonably well groomed, clean, and dressed?

Restraints and bedsores. Residents physically or medically restrained or suffering bedsores spells trouble.

Location. The more the family can visit, the better. The squeaky wheel gets the grease. Nurses pay more attention to residents who do not appear to be forgotten or abandoned.

PATIENTS' RIGHTS

The federal Nursing Home Reform Act (NHRA) applies to any home that has Medicare or Medicaid patients, which includes almost all nursing homes. The NHRA requires that a patient Bill of Rights be given to residents and their families. The most important rights include an individualized treatment plan, to see all of one's clinical records, to complain and be free from reprisal, to send and receive uncensored mail and to make private calls, to refuse treatment, and *not* to be physically or chemically restrained except to prevent physical harm, and then only upon instruction of a doctor.

We cannot stress the importance of the right not to be restrained except under very limited circumstances. In some nursing homes, patients are routinely tied to their chairs by their arms or tied to their bed. Considerable medical evidence indicates that this actually *increases* the incidence of injuries, as patients struggle against restraints, get caught in the restraining devices, or are simply left unattended.

LAW AND COSTS

A patient with mental capacity can check in. If not, there might be a hassle. Best to have a health care power of attorney giving the agent that power and, even then, some states require that a guardianship be obtained.

As to costs, nursing homes are quite expensive, up to $130,000 a year. Medicare doesn't pay. For those who qualify, the costs are covered by Medicaid. Many folks who aren't poor when they enter the nursing home soon run out of money. They then qualify for Medicaid. If you think you or a relative might qualify for Medicaid, contact an elder law attorney. The law of Medicaid eligibility is complicated. Get professional help.

Part Eight

Preparing For the Worst
of Times

31

Estate Planning: An Overview

"Estate planning" smacks of an old English novel,
anxious heirs sitting before a roaring fireplace, and an
elderly lawyer fumbling papers. Did Old Codger really
mean to cut out his son in favor of his new, young wife?
Did the new wife forge his signature? Did she just wink
at her tennis coach? Only 400 pages to go!

Do you need an estate plan? Well you certainly need a will. If you don't, your assets will be distributed according to the *intestate* law of your state, the legislature's best guess on what you probably would want. Most goes to spouses and children and then to other relatives.

There are short-comings with intestacy laws.

- They don't give any money to charity.
- They give a lot of your money to your second spouse and less to your children from your first marriage.
- They don't give money to unmarried life partners, of any orientation.
- They treat all kids the same even though some might have special needs.
- They give money to your ungrateful, drug addict child.

If you have minor children, you can appoint a guardian for them if you die.

Even if most of your assets will be passed by joint ownership or trusts you should have a will because it's almost certain that not all your assets will pass that way. Like your jewelry, stamp collection, and vinyl records.

LETTER OF INSTRUCTION

If you have a will or even if you don't, later this evening sit down and write a list of your passwords, where your important documents are, and where, if you have one, is your safe deposit box. If you have a secret room in your house, as they do in English novels, explain how to get in it.

AVOIDING PROBATE

What is probate? It's a court process where someone, called an executor in some states or personal representative in other states, is appointed to gather the decedent's (the dead person) assets, pay the bills, such as their credit card balance, and distribute what's left according to the will or by intestacy if you didn't write a will.

To avoid probate, die without owning anything. You can spend it all while you are alive or you can make lifetime gifts, set up joint accounts, buy life insurance, and put your money in a trust. You may have a good reason for doing these things, but avoiding probate should not be why you do so. Probate is not a big deal. It has been simplified in many states. And there is one major advantage of probate: your assets will be distributed under court supervision. Any disputes will be handled by a judge.

Don't confuse avoiding probate with avoiding estate taxes. The IRS will be on to you even if your assets don't go through probate.

ESTATE TAXES

Not to worry, they kick in only on estates over $11 million. If you have more than $11 million, good for you. Now put this book down and call a really good estate planning lawyer.

PROBLEMS WITH GIFTS OR BEQUESTS
TO TEENS, MINORS, AND THE MENTALLY
DISABLED

There is always the "nose ring" problem. You don't want your grandchild to get another one. Instead of leaving them money in a will, set up a trust so their inheritance can only be used for their education or medical emergencies. They can get their hands on the money only after they finally grow up. Like at age 40—make that 60.

Neither minors nor those who are mentally disabled have the legal right to make contracts, such as signing a lease. For them, an inheritance creates a host of problems. A trust is the answer. A trust can hold the money and the trustee can use the money in whatever way is best for the trust beneficiary. If the beneficiary is a person with an intellectual disability and is receiving governmental assistance, an inheritance may reduce that assistance. A specially designed trust can solve this problem.

In the next chapter we'll discuss lifetime gifts, joint ownership, life insurance, and IRAs. Remember we raise issues for you that you should be concerned about, not to do; this isn't a self-help book.

Trying to avoid probate can be overdone. Jay Leno was talking to folks about how they can avoid taxes. One man explained, "I quit my job, got rid of my house and car, and spent all my savings. The IRS will never get anything from me."

"Wow! You sure did show them!"

32

Gifts, Joint Ownership, Life Insurance, IRAs, and Living Trusts

Avoid probate, die broke.

LIFETIME GIFTS

Giving is one of life's joys and, better still, there are few tax consequences.

- Recipients of gifts pay no taxes on them.
- Gifts to recognized charities are tax deductible under federal and many state laws.

There is tax problem with appreciated assets, such as property and stocks. Passed at death, the beneficiary gets a stepped-up basis. If you bought land for $10,000 and it is worth $15,000 when you die, your heir's basis is $15,000. The $5,000 gain is never taxed. But if you give that land to someone, that person takes on your basis of $10,000. Sorry, but that is just the way it is. If you're giving away more than $11 million there are estate tax consequences. Talk to your accountant and your attorney. This is no time for DIY.

Large gifts to minors and individuals who have a mental disability can create problems. Before you write that check, "check" with a lawyer. Minors, those under age 18, do not have contractual capacity and gifts to them can create legal problems. In addition, the money may reduce the amount your very smart grandchild receives in college scholarships and loans. Talk to your lawyer.

There are special trusts that are a way to make gifts for available for educational expenses. The most popular are known as "Section 529 plans" after the section of the Internal Revenue Code providing favorable tax treatment. Check with your accountant, bank, or broker.

Use trusts for really big gifts to support your grandchildren's education. We'll tell you how in the next chapter.

LIFE INSURANCE

Beneficiaries collect the death benefit by simply presenting the death certificate to the insurance company. Probate, even in the best of cases, takes time. Proceeds from life insurance policies may come in handy. The proceeds from life insurance do not pass through the estate and are usually not reachable by creditors.

Some will advise you to cancel life insurance policies because your kids are grown and to buy long-term care policies instead. Think about doing that. As we age, the need for insurance may shift from providing for our families at death to providing for ourselves at incapacity.

There are companies that will buy your policy. Cash now, cash to them when you die. We don't know much about them, but we note that you may be "paying" a lot to get money now rather than your beneficiary getting money when you die. But $30,000 paid to you may be worth more to you than your beneficiary getting $50,000 a few years from now when you die.

JOINT OWNERSHIP

Some tout joint ownership of property and stocks as the best way of avoiding probate. However, except for less valuable items, such as a car and relatively small bank accounts, joint ownership may not be a good idea.

- There are several forms of joint ownership; only some have a "right of survivorship," which vests title in one joint owner at the time the other dies. Without such a survivorship aspect, joint ownership does not avoid probate: at the death of one joint owner, his or her share stays in his or her estate.

- Joint ownership presents problems if both owners die at the same time, and may have adverse income, gift, and estate tax consequences.

- Joint ownership means giving up unfettered control over the asset.

- As long as property is in joint ownership, the creditors of the other owner can reach it.

- In some states, joint ownership won't even speed transfer of assets upon death. Some states automatically freeze joint accounts until tax officials can check things out. (Bank employees read the obits.)

ANNUITIES, IRAS, AND ROTH IRA

IRAs and Roth IRAs are good ways to pass money; ownership passes to the designed beneficiaries without going through probate and the money is not available to creditors of the estate. With a traditional IRA (or a 401(k) and similar retirement plans) one must start withdrawing money in the year after the year in which one turns 72. (Don't ask. Even better, ask an accountant.) In the first years this means a withdrawal of about 4% of the total amount, going to about 8% at the age of 88. You'll pay income taxes on these amounts.

A Roth IRA is a good deal:

No required withdrawals. Tax free withdrawals (after the first five years).

Unlike traditional IRAs, contributions to Roth IRAs are not deductible when they are made. You can convert a traditional

IRA or other retirement account into a Roth IRA, but income taxes must be paid at the time.

When an IRA, 401(k), Roth IRA, or other retirement account owner dies, the rules get complicated unless the owner's surviving spouse is named as beneficiary. Talk to your lawyer about how to leave an IRA to anyone who is not your spouse.

BENEFICIARY DESIGNATIONS— POOR MAN'S TRUSTS

POD (payable on death), TOD (transfer on death), or ITF (in trust) accounts transfer funds (or perhaps property) on death of the owner—but do not convey any right to the money or property while you are still alive. When you die, the money or property goes to the beneficiary and avoids probate.

LIVING TRUSTS

You may have read about living trusts and how they are the best thing since sliced bread. Well, they can be helpful. Assets in a living trust avoid probate because the trust, not you, owns the assets in the trust. Also, if you become disabled—let's be blunt—if you develop dementia, whoever you named to take over the trust can manage the money in the trust and use it to take care of you. But it costs money to set up a living trust, and you have to go through the hassle of transferring assets, like your bank accounts or mutual funds, to the trust. More on these later.

33

Trusts

Remember the Shmoos of the Li'l Abner comic strip?
They were marvelous. They would play with the
kids, clean the house, and then cook themselves
for dinner. Trusts are a little like that.
They can do many things.

We've talked a lot about trusts. It's time to bring you up to speed on the what, how, and why of trusts. First, some vocabulary (you won't have to use them in a sentence or even spell them).

The trustors, grantors, or settlors give money or property to a trustee (a bank, a friend, or, as we will see with Living Trusts, themselves) to be managed and used in trust for the benefit of the beneficiary (a spouse, a charity, a minor child, a relative, or, as we will see, themselves). The remainder beneficiary is the person or charity that takes whatever is left when the trust ends. The money or property is to be used as directed by the trust instrument, which will say who are the beneficiaries, how, when, and to whom the trust will give money, and when the trust will end.

You can create trusts while you are alive, called inter vivos trusts, or in your will—called testamentary trusts. You can even create a standby trust during your life, and fund it at your death by a gift in your will.

TRUSTS FOR PERSONS WITH MENTAL DISABILITIES OR MENTAL ILLNESS

If you want to leave money to a person with a mental disability or mental illness, you need to act carefully—and call a lawyer. Income paid to such folks may make them ineligible for public assistance. A special needs trust solves this problem: the beneficiary can receive benefits for education, extra therapy, furniture, paid companionship, and trips to Disneyland but nothing for food or shelter. Uh? Your lawyer will explain how this works.

A few things to consider no matter what kind of trust you create.

REVOCABLE OR IRREVOCABLE?

If you create a revocable trust, if you change your mind, you can terminate the trust and get your property back. However, your creditors can reach a revocable trust, and you have to report all the trust income on your federal income tax return. As for irrevocable trusts, ask your accountant or your lawyer about the tax consequences and other implications of irrevocable trusts.

CONFLICT BETWEEN CURRENT AND LATER BENEFICIARIES

In English novels trustees are tottering old men who fall in love with their shy, beautiful ward, who is, in turn, madly in love with a poor but struggling—yet destined for greatness—doctor. But it's hard to be a trustee even if your ward doesn't run off with a younger man.

Trustees are in a bind. They have obligations both to the current beneficiary and to the remainder beneficiaries who take what's left when the trust ends. If the trustee is too generous to the current beneficiary, the trustee may be sued by the remainder beneficiaries. Help!

You can avoid that problem with language in the trust that ex-

plains that you want or don't want the trustee to favor the beneficiary over the remainder beneficiary. Your lawyer will know how
to word the trust so that the trustee has the power to do what you
want him, her, or it—it might be a bank—to do.

Powers of the Trustee

What the trustee can and can't do is determined by the powers
you give him, her, or it and by state law. Your lawyer will go over
the choices you have.

Choosing the Trustee

Banks will not agree to act as a trustee unless the trust has a lot
of money or very valuable assets in it. For the rest of us, a spouse,
a child, grandchild, or other relative will have to do as trustee.
You can name more than one person as trustee. That is often the
case if you more than one child. Should the trustee be paid? Maybe. Consider the trustee's relation to the beneficiaries, financial
skills, age in relation to beneficiaries, and geographical proximity.
Always name an alternative or successor trustee, just in case.

*A woman created a trust and named her beloved manicurist
as the trustee. Unfortunately, the manicurist didn't know
finances and lost the entire million dollars.*

You can read this story broadly (trust your mind more than
your heart) or narrowly (don't trust your manicurist).

34

Living Trusts

In the comedy Raising Arizona, a baby is kidnapped and one mean-looking bounty-hunter approaches the father offering to find his baby.

"Why should I hire you?" the father asks. "The police are on it."

"If ya want to find your baby, ask me. If ya want to find a donut, ask the police."

We can make it fit.

> *"If ya want to find a free donut, go to a living trust seminar. If ya want a living trust, go to a lawyer"*

Today's hot item, often sold at free breakfasts. The price ranges from $900 to $1,500. The pitch?

- You will avoid probate and won't need a will! Kinda true.
  - If you have property outside of the trust, (and you probably will), probate and a will will be needed.
- You won't need a guardianship! Kinda true.
  - Your spouse or trustee will take over your finances if you can't. But your planning is not done; far more important is a health care power of attorney.
- Nine out of ten people who purchase living trusts don't need one. True.

There are cheaper and easier ways of accomplishing the same things, but let's take a look at what a living trust might be.

THE LIVING TRUST
OF JANE AND JOHN DOE

The assets of this Trust shall be used for the benefit of Jane and John Doe, husband and wife, and shall be administered by them. In the event that they become incapable of administering this Trust, it shall be administered by their son, Adam, and their daughter, Eve, or, if they cannot, by the First National Bank. At the death of either Jane or John, this Trust shall become irrevocable. Thereafter, the assets of the Trust will be used for the benefit of the survivor. At the death of the survivor, the assets remaining in the Trust shall be distributed in equal parts to the then surviving children of Jane and John.

Of course things are much more complicated than that but, as lawyers love to do, let's parse the language.

"The assets"

They can move as much of their money and other property into the trust as they like. Titles to real property must be changed. Lawyers know how.

"for the benefit of Jane and John Doe, husband and wife, and shall be administered by them"

Not much has changed. Jane and John continue to manage their financial affairs as before, but now, as to property in the trust, must sign as "trustees."

"At the death of either, this Trust shall become irrevocable."

Until the death of either, the Trust is revocable. They can change their minds and take everything out. Income it earns will go on their individual return. Once a Trust becomes irrevocable, will become a separate tax entity, will have to get its own tax number, and will have to pay its own taxes. And the surviving spouse cannot revoke the trust and cannot change who gets the remainder when the Trust ends. Why would you want that? Because you can never be sure of who your spouse, after a respectful time of mourning, might fall in love with, marry, and name as the beneficiary of the trust rather than your children.

> *"In the event that Jane and John become incapable of administering this Trust, it shall be administered by their son, Adam, and their daughter, Eve, or, if they cannot, by the First National Bank."*

This acts like a power of attorney for finances.

> *"At the death of the survivor, the assets remaining in the Trust shall be distributed in equal parts to the children of Jane and John."*

Here the living trust is acting like a will. Clear enough, but lawyers spot problems; that's why they get the big bucks. What if the daughter, Eve, has two children and dies before her parents? Do the grandkids get anything? If they're to get Eve's share, and one grandchild is disabled and can't work, should get both get the same amount? In the simplest of language lurk legal problems.

> *Creating a living trust is a big deal. Living trusts change lives. Free breakfasts present one of life's hard choices: coffee and a donut or your family's wellbeing.*

How about going on the Web and doing your own? You'll need legal help, now or when your living will goes south.

35

Health Care Directives

Every human being of adult years and of sound mind has a
right to determine what shall be done with his body . . . .
JUDGE BENJAMIN CARDOZO (1914)

As long as you have your wits, you can decide your health care.
You can so as you please; reject life-saving treatment, refuse to
eat your spinach, and stay up late (if you're an adult of sound
mind). If you become legally incapacitated, everything changes.
You'll need to create documents that will help others decide for
you.

LIVING WILL

Living wills were once the Next Big Thing. You signed a document that told everyone how you wanted to be treated in case you
were dying. Usually that meant, "pull the plug." Sounds good, except we have learned that living wills usually don't work. they are
typically ignored. Despite the living will, the family insists that
you aren't dying—not yet, and doctors generally do what your
family wants. Also the doctor doesn't want to follow a form that
you signed years ago. The doctor wants to discuss your situation
with your family and decide on what kind of treatment, if any,
makes sense given your age and medical condition.

HEALTH CARE POWER OF ATTORNEY

Forget the living will. Instead sign a health care power of attorney. Every state has a law that lets you name someone to make health care decisions for you if you come mentally incapacitated. Although the document goes by different names in different states, all permit you to name a person you trust to make the right medical decisions for you *anytime* you can't, such as if you develop dementia. You also have the right to give some instructions to that person as to how you want to be treated in case you are near death.

Before you sign a health care power of attorney, you have two big decisions to make.

Who should you pick? If you are married, you will likely name your spouse. You will also name a back-up in case you spouse is not mentally up to the job or is dead. Usually a child or grandchild is named as back-up. Name only one person to serve at a time. You don't want a two or three of your children fighting over what kind of health care should be provided to you.

What powers? You probably should include all the powers that state law permits, including the power to not start or to end life-sustaining treatment. But you may think otherwise. If so, tailor the powers to match your values. As they say, it's your life, you can do what you want.

Where to get a health care power of attorney. The Web has forms, many forms, but it's wiser to have a lawyer draft it. You want a document that is familiar and makes sense to your doctor. Your lawyer will know how to do that.

If you don't take our advice and don't sign a health care power of attorney, most states now have surrogacy statutes that automatically appoint someone to make medical decisions for you when you can't, starting with the spouse, then children, and so on. But don't depend on state law. Sign a health care power of attorney.

No discussion of healthcare documents would be complete without:

DO NOT RESUSCITATE (DNR)

How many times on television have you seen some "doctor" declare a Code Blue, start pounding the patient's chest, place paddles on the patient, call "clear," and stand back, smiling with relief as the patient's heart starts beating? How wonderful. Unfortunately, in real life 80% of patients whose hearts stop beating die. Many who survive soon die of other causes. Some survive with broken ribs. Knowing that, many folks who are suffering from a terminal illness do not want to be resuscitated. So they sign a DNR (Do Not Resuscitate) order, which is usually available in the hospital, that directs health care workers to back off and let nature do its work.

If you don't want to be "rescued" at home by paramedics, which is their job, sign a specialized DNR that tells the paramedics to leave the paddles in the ambulance and let you die. State laws and procedures vary widely on when and how DNRs work. But if you have a DNR, be sure folks know about it. Post the directive where they'll see it, and wear a bracelet that says you have a DNR. If you fear that the paramedics will probably save you anyway, tell your caregiver not to call them too quickly.

Documents can take you only so far. Even the best-drafted will be somewhat ambiguous, and family disputes may arise. *Family conversations* are key in assuring your wishes will be carried out. Have that difficult discussion so that whoever has to make health decisions for you has the comfort of knowing that they are doing what you wanted even if it leads to your death. Of course, this assumes that you know what you want. So sit down and figure out what your wishes are.

Part Nine

The Final Curtain

36

Death in the Family

"So you're not interested in buying the deluxe coffin for your mother," smiles the mortician, "how about a nice pillow?"

If a relative dies there's a lot to be done. It's a blessing; it will help get you through the first weeks.

FUNERAL HOMES AND BURIAL

Funeral homes can be called at any hour. They take care of official notifications and arrange for copies of the official death certificate needed in notifying insurance companies, Social Security, and retirement plans. Obituaries in local papers can be arranged by the funeral home at a modest cost.

Take a look through the person's papers. There may be burial and funeral instructions. Hopefully, they had a "When I Die" file which holds wills, legal documents, and passwords.

Funerals are expensive, and there are strong psychological pressures to overspend, not wanting to appear "cheap" and desiring to show love.

Don't agree on the first visit; go home and think how the person would want money to be spent—college for grandkids or Hawaii for you—you deserve it.

Cremation is less expensive. Ashes can be scattered where permitted. Cremation is more widespread than ever before, chosen by about half of Americans.

Autopsies might disclose unknown genetic diseases, or they might disclose that Granddad wasn't suffering from the genetic disease his family feared. They're required if the cause of death is suspicious or unknown, and depending on state law, in some other cases.

Organ donations are wonderful gifts. They relieve the suffering of others, the ultimate play it forward. Even if the decedent left no instructions, usually the family can authorize the donation. Some have religious objections, and some object in the mistaken belief that they would delay the funeral, prevent a viewing, or increase the funeral cost. Generally, they don't.

Bills. Let things settle before paying the person's bills, particularly medical and nursing home bills. If the estate is to be probated, the estate will pay the bills; if there is a trust, the trustee will.

As a general rule, only the person (or his or her estate) who received the service is liable to pay the bill. Generally, family members (children and spouses) are not required to pay the bills. This may be different in the community property states (Arizona, California, Idaho, Louisiana, Nevada, New Mexico, Texas, Washington, and Wisconsin).

Some bills may be bogus. Scam artists take advantage of a family's distress by sending bills from the Hot Times Massage or Studs at Your Service. You're so embarrassed that you quickly and quietly send them a check.

Continue to pay ongoing bills, such as rent, utilities, and, yes, the lawyer's fees for probate. If these bills are not paid, the services will stop.

Notifications. Notify life insurance companies. Maybe the company where the person worked maintained life insurance on its employees. Close their internet accounts.

Call Social Security. Folks who might be entitled to benefits include dependent children, dependent parents, surviving spouses, and even if the couple was not married, the survivor if they had, or adopted, a child together.

There is a small Social Security death benefit for surviving spouses. It is not a lot of money. It's been stuck at $255 for decades.

37

Probate

*Probate is boring; we'll start with a murder,
and then you can stop reading.*

In 1889 Elmer (a name which has not survived the ravages of time) poisoned his grandfather. He feared that the old gent would rewrite his will and leave him nothing. Not wishing to become a disgruntled heir he took matters into his own hands, but when he showed up in court to collect his money he was met with "Hey, wait a minute, Elmer, you murdered the guy. You can't take under his will."

"Says who?"

Thus opens one of the most famous of cases, *Riggs v. Palmer.* Now it seems self-evident that a murderer should not be allowed to inherit from his victim, but it wasn't so easy in 1889.

There were seven judges. Three thought Elmer should get the money. If he committed the crime, they argued, he should be tried in criminal court where his guilt would have to be established "beyond a reasonable doubt" and not in probate court, where guilt would be established by a mere "preponderance of the evidence."

The other four judges thought differently and held that murderers cannot inherit from their victim. That's the law today. In one of the great phrases in the law, the judges wrote "No one should profit from their own wrong."

Knowing the world as we do that's more inspirational than descriptive.

In Dickens' day probate ruined families (and enriched lawyers) and inspired his great novel *Bleak House*. Things have changed radically but "probate" still retains its bad reputation. There are several current books titled *Avoid Probate*. In chapter 32 we discussed many ways to avoid probate: give your money away, buy life insurance, set up joint accounts, create trusts, designate beneficiaries in your IRA, and, perhaps not everyone's first choice, die broke.

Thankfully, probate ain't what it used to be. Most people with large estates have created trusts to handle their stocks and bonds, real property, and bank accounts. Trusts do not go through probate; when the person dies the trustee continues to manage the assets in accord with the trust instrument.

As to the things around the house, they can simply be divided: Jane gets the sofa, John takes the 60-inch television. However, there may be things that have particular significance to family members, such as paintings, family photos, jewelry, and dolls. Hopefully who gets what has already been agreed on; if not, go slowly. The future of the family may hang in the balance. More families are destroyed by fights over these items than over money.

"I know there are some things we would all like to have to remember Mom. Let's not fight over them. Remember the well-being of our family is more important than who gets this vase or that Tiffany lamp."

Property with titles. Cars, houses, land, stocks, and bonds have "title." Before the family can sell them, the title must be rewritten. Usually that's not much of a problem.

If the title shows a co-owner, indicating the right of survivorship, the co-owner simply shows the death certificate to the appropriate official. With cars, the appropriate official is the DMV, with land and houses it is the county recorder or clerk. For stocks, bonds, and brokerage and bank accounts, simply present a death certificate at the appropriate office.

If the title is *only* in the decedent's name, probate may be needed. However, if not much property is involved, most states allow for quick and inexpensive probate, usually involving simply filling out a form and attaching a death certificate.

When do you need probate? If your will directs gifts to charities or relatives, if it provides specific property go to specific people, or if you have a lot of property or, particularly, if you have a business. Without a will, the business will probably fall apart.

Probate is simply a court proceeding where your assets are assembled, bills are paid, and what's left is distributed according to the will or, if there is no will, according the state's intestacy law, which is the legislature's best guess about how you would want things distributed. One advantage of probate is that a court administers the distribution rather than a trustee. Trustees act on their own and aren't accountable to you—unless you want to sue them. Many states have expedited probate procedures.

Full-blown probates are time consuming and expensive. We'll leave it up to your lawyer to give you the details.

You might have noticed that the language of the law is rather dull and lacks literary flare—"plaintiffs," "wards" "codicils"—but then come disgruntled heirs.

DISGRUNTLED HEIRS

Will contests are rare, but disgruntled heirs may make trouble. They're the folks who would get more under the law of intestacy than they will get under the will or trust. They include:

Surviving Spouses

Unless there is a prenuptial agreement, and no matter what the will says, surviving spouses are entitled to something: often a third of the estate (half, in some jurisdictions, or a flat dollar amount, in others).

Forgotten Children.

Natural, adopted, and illegitimate children not named in the will can argue that the decedent didn't mean to cut them out, only forgot them. This might include children born, and spouses married, after the will was written. The claim is that the decedent didn't mean to cut them out. State law may take care of that claim, providing in many cases that such "pretermitted" heirs take a share equal to that they would have received if no will had been written.

Heirs Who Suspect Lack of Capacity

If the testator lost legal capacity before signing the will (or trust), it is invalid and the estate passes under the intestacy law or a prior valid will.

Heirs Who Suspect Undue Influence

Large gifts to nurses, neighbors, and TV evangelists are suspect. Was the person in a position to assert control over the testator by threats or by withholding care?

Heirs Who Suspect Murder

You already know "you can't profit from your own wrong," If Sis can prove Bro did in dear old Dad, he can't get a nickel, so there's more for Sis. Someone always profits from wrong.

You knew that.

38

Ending Life: Pulling Plugs, Suicide, and Death with Dignity

I have been half in love with easeful Death . . .

To cease upon the midnight with no pain.

JOHN KEATS

PULLING PLUGS

Your uncle is in a very bad way. His doctor asks your permission to shut off his breathing tube or to take him off his feeding and hydration tubes.

You can't prepare for this. Living wills and health care powers of attorney, however, help, as do prior frank discussions with your uncle about the possibility of this occurring.

All of that is fine and easy for us to say. But one night, reality may suddenly crash in and you find yourself in a hospital hallway, busy with doctors and nurses, pretty well ignored, and it's no longer theoretical, and your uncle's doctor is asking "Well?"

A few things to think about now, before that night.

- Removing tubes is not killing your uncle; it is letting nature take its course.

- Showing love may mean keeping your uncle alive or it may mean letting him die.

- Get other family members involved and listen to their opinions. It is important that it be a family decision, not just yours.

- You will feel horrible no matter what you decide. There is not a "good" choice, just a choice between "bad" outcomes. Pulling the breathing plug is not like turning off the light. Your uncle will struggle, and it is best if you are not in the room. That is not how you want to remember him.

- Removing feeding and hydration tubes is peaceful. Your uncle will die of dehydration, not starving, in about ten days. Efforts will be made to relieve dry mouth and thirst. Nurses assure us that this is the best death.

Speaking of *feeding and hydration tubes: it far easier to keep them out than it is to get them out.* If a loved one is in a nursing home and the staff recommends such tubes, think long and hard before authorizing them. They have a financial interest in keeping the patient alive, no matter how dismal the prospects and no matter how painful the condition. Once the tubes are in, it may take a court order—or at least an extraordinary amount of effort and angst—to get them removed.

DEATH WITH DIGNITY

In 1998 an Oregon woman, dying of breast cancer, became the first person to use Oregon's Death with Dignity Law. She died peacefully in her sleep, at home, surrounded by her family. Her physician prescribed a lethal medication; five minutes later she was asleep, thirty minutes later, dead.

In 2019 an elderly man in a retirement facility invited his friends to his death. It was actually festive and he, like Huck Finn, heard all the nice things people say at funerals.

Helping another to commit suicide is a crime. It's not a defense that the victim wanted to die, asked for the help, was in great pain, or would have died anyway—or that the act was motivated by love and compassion.

Death with Dignity laws create a narrow exception. Doctors can prescribe, but not administer, drugs that kill. The patient must take the final step and self-administer the lethal drugs.

Oregon was the first to pass the legislation in 1994 and now California (2015), Colorado (2016), District of Columbia (2017), Hawaii (2019), Maine (2019), New Jersey (2019), Vermont (2013), and Washington (2008) have as well.

Most of these laws require two physicians to certify that the patient (1) has, to a reasonable medical certainty, no more than six months to live, (2) is competent, (3) has been informed of alternatives to suicide (hospice, pain control), and (4) is making a voluntary choice in requesting the lethal prescription.

If the patient is depressed or suffering mental illness, no prescription will be written. Nor will one be written until at least fifteen days after the initial request, and only then if the patient repeats the request.

If all of these steps are properly taken, the physicians will not be civilly or criminally liable for writing the prescription, and, if the patient takes the medications, it will not be deemed a suicide for life insurance purposes.

Very few have used these laws. Those who have are about equally divided by sex, overwhelmingly white, well-educated, and financially comfortable. Most made the choice, not to avoid pain, but rather out of a desire to control their lives. Most had terminal cancer or Lou Gehrig's disease.

Is Assisted Suicide a Good Idea?

There are very convincing arguments on both sides. In support, being human entails the right to captain one's own destiny. Why shouldn't you have the right to end your own life and to seek medical help to do so? Why shouldn't you be allowed to avoid the great pain and expense generally associated with stays in the ICU?

Another less obvious argument in favor of physician-assisted suicide: it may actually *reduce* suicide. Many, suffering from chronic illness, fear that it will eventually lead to unbearable suffering and that, when it does come, they will no longer have the ability to end it themselves. In panic, they take their own lives. The mere promise that, if that time arrives, there will be someone there for them could stay their hand.

But there are strong philosophical and religious concerns against condoning any form of suicide. No one should play God, the guiding principle of medicine is "first, do no harm," and legalized suicide, even if not widespread, will lead to a general cheapening of human life.

There are practical concerns as well: if assisted suicide is available, how can relatives be prevented from dumping expensive or inconvenient relatives? From accelerating their inheritance?

The major argument in favor of these laws is that people should have the freedom to choose to end their life and die with dignity.

Why must one have a terminable illness before they have that freedom? Why deny a consenting adult medical help in ending a life made unbearable by a severe, chronic, fatal illness, such as Lou Gehrig's Disease, simply because that disease has not yet progressed to the "terminal stage"?

Condoning suicide, it is argued, may slowly lead to involuntary euthanasia. The state acknowledges that some lives aren't worth living, and the next step may be to put severely disabled individuals "out of their misery." Fanciful?

You may have heard the argument that the elderly have a "duty" to step aside. A group of severely disabled individuals, fiercely opposed to physician-assisted suicide, calls itself "Not Dead Yet." We, as a society, have too much history with eugenics and social engineering to be trusted with this tool, or so the argument goes.

DOUBLE EFFECT PAIN MEDICATION

Pain relief, which has the *unintended* result of causing death, is neither suicide nor euthanasia. Physicians prescribe morphine for certain painful illnesses; as the pain increases, so, too, the dosages. Increased dosages increase suppression of breathing and heart rate, and may eventually lead to death. This is known as a treatment's "double effect."

SUICIDE

Suicide is when you kill yourself. It is final, very final. Shakespeare nailed it:

> Here lies the water, here stands the man, if the man goes to the water, and drown himself, he goes, mark you that, but if the water comes to him and drown him, he drowns not himself. —*Hamlet*

If a friend seems to be considering suicide, don't change the subject. Instead, ask direct questions.

"Are you OK?"

"Are you thinking about suicide?"

"Have you made a plan?"

If there are guns in the house, take them. And take a look at our chapter on depression. Call the National Suicide Prevention Lifeline: 800-273-8255.

There are how-to suicide books and there are advocates. But consider:

- Most survivors of suicide attempts go on to live good lives.
- There are many new and promising treatments to deal with depression. Many are drug free, like going for walks or hanging out with friends.
- Almost all pain can be alleviated by proper medication.
- Suicide of a loved one is the hardest death to get over. You'll

be sentencing your loved ones to a life of guilt: "Was this my fault? What should I have done?"

Finally, let's talk brass tacks. If your choice is to crash your car, you may go out as a murderer. If you choose a gun, it's messy. Who will find your bloody body? Who will be cursed forever by the image?

If you are feeling suicidal, talk to family, friends, and spiritual advisers. If you don't, you do them a double wrong: your death and your cruel denial of their opportunity to reach out to comfort you.

39

Hospice

Go gentle into that good night.

"Hospice."

Many cringe.

"I'm not going, I'm not giving up, I'm not dead yet."

Hospice has a bad rap. But it's wonderful. The major regret of families who have had a loved one in hospice is that they waited too long. Their loved one suffered unnecessary pain and inadequate care.

We'll offer some advice if you're visiting a loved one in hospice or if you are a patient there. Before that, some basics.

Hospice service can be obtained at home. A hospice team will visit and provide care and much needed respite for caregivers. Hospital beds and other supplies are available.

Hospice is essentially free (the good news) for patients on Medicare if their physician believes they will die within the next six months (which is the bad news). Medicaid and private insurance may pay as well. And there is private pay.

Hospice works to control pain. Drugs designed to cure the patient are limited, and the focus is on comfort, not cure. Cutting down on drugs often makes the patient better, as drugs can interact badly, and due to this some patients walk out.

Hospice care is usually by a team, including a nurse, a social worker, a spiritual counselor, and perhaps a volunteer. A medical director, a physician expert in end-of-life issues, supervises.

Hospice works with the family. The spiritual advisors, the nurses, and the social workers know what families are going through, the confusion, heartbreak, uncertainty, and perhaps guilt. The families are not alone. Often hospice workers form close bonds with family members.

Not all hospices are alike. Visit at least two and what you like and don't like will jump out. Location is one critical factor, as visits are essential. The VA has hospices for veterans. You might want to list some questions to ask; this chapter will help.

VISITING A LOVED ONE

You'll be distressed to learn the patient isn't eating and is sleeping too much. Both are to be expected. The body is slowly shutting down, it doesn't need much food, and forcing the patient to eat may cause problems. As to sleep, they need it.

Visiting is critical. We all fear dying alone. A nurse tells of a dying veteran whose last wish was for his family to go across the hall to sit with a fellow veteran who had no visitors.

Talk to the patient. There may be unpleasant things, unsettled scores. If the patient doesn't bring them up maybe you should, but it's a good idea to ask permission.

"Is it OK if we talk about the time I moved out?"

Hearing and touch are the last things to go. Your loved one may seem asleep, may seem about to die. Hold their hand and talk.

"Remember our trip to Paris? Teaching our granddaughter how to ride a bike? Your friends and family are here. We will all miss you, but we will all be fine. You can go now."

In her book, *Final Exam,* Dr. Pauline Chen writes "Being with the dying allows us to nurture our best humanistic tendencies." And it eases our own fear of death.

BEING IN HOSPICE

You make all the difference. If you curse your fate and feel sorry for yourself, things will go badly for you, for your loved ones, and for your caregivers.

At one point in your life you might have come across Dylan Thomas' searing advice to his dying father:

Do not go gentle into that good night, . . .
Rage, rage against the dying of the light.

It's doubtful his dad paid much attention, and you shouldn't either. Far better to listen to John Keats and go gentle into that good night:

I have been half in love with easeful Death, . . .
To cease upon the midnight with no pain . . .

As with birth, death is natural. It is time to reflect rather than fight. Hospice workers talk about how close they have come to patients, how much they have learned about life listening to their stories. As a patient what a wonderful gift you can give. Hospice is a two-way street.

Of course this does not mean a smiley face. This will be a hard time. Old scores may come up and be resolved. You'll probably want to talk about your fears, your concerns for your family, and your death. Family members will be reluctant to bring these matters up; you should.

"I'm afraid."

"I'm worried about how you guys will get on."

Hospice isn't a place, it's a philosophy. *Make peace with death.*

We all know we're going to die but not really. We deny, we

make jokes. Woody Allen said, "I'm OK with dying, I just don't want to be there when it happens."

Once we have made peace with death our lives become better. No more background noise, no more looking over our shoulder.

Death is going to win. The question is when.

To learn more about hospice, go to "Go Gentle into that Good Night" at Gogentle.org.

40

Being There and Mourning

"It is not death, but dying which is terrible."
HENRY FIELDING

One of the many "bummers" of getting older is death—of acquaintances, friends, loved ones, and, yes, even yourself. As unwelcome as it is, death will come. It cares not what you think. How you respond to it, however, is up to you

Dying alone is a constant fear. If a loved one is dying, go visit, be there even if you don't want to be, even if your thoughts are not loving or profound, even if you don't have time. Make time. If not, you'll feel guilty later. To flee sickness and death is instinctive. There may be resentment stemming from prior wrongs; there may be self-pity from being left alone; there may be unpleasant unfinished business. But ignore those negative memories and do the right thing. You'll be glad you did.

Will they know you're there? Better than knowing you're not. Hearing goes last: whispering memories, offering encouragement, and, to break the emotional intensity of those moments, telling a great story.

Oscar Wilde on his deathbed said, "The wallpaper in this room is terrible. One of us has to go."

Voltaire, a committed atheist, on his deathbed, was encouraged to denounce the Devil. "I've made enough enemies."

We're told that mourning is a process, with marked stages and with final goals. No doubt that is true for many people, but not for all. Don't beat yourself up if you think you aren't doing it right or not feeling the things you think you should.

Some grieve before the death and experience the actual death with relief. And there is the background question, "What I am to do now?" Dylan Thomas's wife wrote a book with the haunting title *Leftover Life to Kill*. Despair mixed with relief; dark, intense moments mixed with daily chores and gossip. Life is always in the *present* tense. Best advice: be with friends, neighbors, and relatives. Talk. Cry. Tell jokes.

An elderly couple sits on the couch. The wife says, "If I die first, you should remarry. If you die first, I'll get a dog."

Why are dogs better than husbands? They don't wake you in the middle of the night and ask, "If I die, will you get a new dog?"

A goal of mourning is not to get over the death but to *relocate* the loved one—to create a different kind of relationship with the person.

"Can you believe what the president said? I wish I could call Mom and get her reaction. What would she say?"

In a marvelous poem, "*Funeral Blues*," W. H. Auden captures how many feel at the death of a loved one, the initial shock, indeed resentment, that the world goes on as before.

Stop all the clocks, cut off the telephone,
Prevent the dog from barking with a juicy bone,
Silence the pianos, and with a muffled drum
Bring out the coffin, let the mourners come.

He ends with the feeling of despair:

The stars are not wanted now; put out every one,
Pack up the moon and dismantle the sun;

Pour away the ocean and sweep up the wood;
For nothing now can ever come to any good.

But maybe not. Years ago Joe Biden's wife and daughter were killed in a car wreck. Later one of his sons died of cancer. No doubt he felt that nothing could ever come to any good. Decades later, as vice president of the United States, he addressed a gathering of mothers and fathers, wives and husbands, and sons and daughters of soldiers who had been killed in Iraq and Afghanistan.

"*I promise you this. There will come a time, I promise you, there will come a time when you think of them, you will smile before you cry.*"

We've come a long way together. When we started we talked about John Quincy Adams and his unsuccessful search for the Ultimate Generalization, one that would explain everything. We were more successful, coming up with the Ultimate Advice, one that would always work. As we part we want to remind you and, indeed, ourselves:

Keep singing.

Useful Websites

AARP aarp.org

Administration for Community Living eldercare.gov

Alzheimer's Association alz.org

Alzheimer's Reading Room (blog) alzheimersreadingroom.
  wordpress.com

BenefitsCheckUp benefitscheckup.org

CareZone carezone.com

Corporation for National and Community Service national
  service.gov

Craigslist craigslist.org

Do Not Call Registry donotcall.gov

Generations United gu.org

Go Gentle into that Good Night gogentle.org

Home Equity Conversion Mortgage (HECM) hud.gov/
  program_offices/housing/sfh/hecm/hecmhome

Lotsa Helping Hands lotsahelpinghands.com

Medicare medicare.gov

National Academy of Elder Law Attorneys (NAELA) naela.org

Pension Benefit Guaranty Corporation pbgc.gov

Savingforcollege.com savingforcollege.com

Social Security ssa.gov

WebMD webmd.com

Index